Greenhouse Gardening

HOW TO BUILD, MAINTAIN AND STOCK
ALL TYPES OF GREENHOUSES

BY JEROME A. EATON

GROSSET
GOOD LIFE
BOOKS

PUBLISHERS • GROSSET & DUNLAP • NEW YORK
A FILMWAYS COMPANY

Acknowledgments

Cover photograph courtesy of Lord & Burnham

The author expresses his appreciation to the following for permission to use their illustrations in this book:
Aluminum Greenhouses Inc.: p. 9 top; Chapin Watermatics, Inc.: p. 33 bottom left; O. Wesley Davidson: p. 51 top right, p. 56 top right, p. 56 bottom left; Gottscho-Schleisner, Inc.: p. 7, p. 10 bottom, p. 15 bottom, p. 36 bottom, p. 66, p. 73, p. 79 top, p. 83, p. 85, p. 87, p. 89, p. 91 top; M. R. Harrison: p. 57 bottom; Humex Ltd.: p. 31 bottom left, p. 43 bottom right; Robert A. Levinson: p. 63 top right; Lord & Burnham: p. 25; Popular Science Publishing Co.: p. 23 top.

Contents

1
The Pleasures
of Gardening under Glass

If you delight in the color and fragrance of flowers and enjoy seeing plants sprout from seed, gain strength and grow to maturity, these pleasures can be yours the year around—if you have a greenhouse. With this useful structure, you can simulate any climate in the world and grow any plant your heart desires, no matter where you live. This seeming miracle is accomplished by very simple means. A greenhouse is essentially a glass box in which you control the amount of light, heat and humidity. With the proper equipment and controls you can establish any climate you want from a desert floor to a tropical jungle or alpine slope. The glass enclosure simply stabilizes the air and keeps your chosen climate from drifting away.

How much work does a greenhouse require?

Don't let your concern about the work required keep you from enjoying the beauty and pleasure that a greenhouse can bring. The amount of time and effort needed depends entirely on the plants you choose to grow. Plants requiring a warm greenhouse call for more attention in order to maintain the various aspects of the climate in their proper proportions. Plants for cut flowers call for a few additional chores beyond those of pot plants. However, with the efforts come the rewards and the choice is yours.

The location you choose for your greenhouse also has a bearing on how much maintenance it will require. If it is not in everyday view it doesn't matter much if there are seasons with little if any color or display, or if some things get a little overgrown, or if the glass is less than spotless. On the other hand, if it is adjacent to the living area where it is, in effect, a part of daily life, it will require more attention. If it is on constant view it pays to keep a succession of blooms coming on the year around and everything should be kept as bright and shining as any other part of the house. But no matter where you put it, be it large or small, cool or warm (you'll read about the differences later on) there is no better way to live intimately with the world of plants than to have a greenhouse of your own.

2
Choosing the Greenhouse That Suits You Best

Suburban living has become such a popular way of life that it is difficult to remember back to the early 1940's when the flight to the suburbs was just beginning in earnest. It was then that the great interest in greenhouse gardening began to grow. Its popularization was also a result of the new industries which had arisen out of World War II having to find new peacetime applications for their newly developed products. Aluminum, plastics and electronics are only three of many that found the greenhouse industry eager to utilize their expertise in developing an inexpensive and efficient product that required a low level of maintenance. Quaint structures still reminiscent of the Victorian era were soon superseded by those of attractive simple design and what had been for centuries a pastime of the privileged class became a hobby for all to enjoy. Just as their appearance underwent drastic change so did the concept of the use of greenhouses benefit from new and creative thinking. No longer considered the work structure relegated to the back of the property line surrounded by stacks of pots, piles of coal, mounds of manure and bins of soil, the greenhouse was soon to become a focal point of the home. In some instances the greenhouse is now a living area where you are surrounded by a green and perfumed environment. In others, one looks out upon a lush tropical scene—even in midwinter—instead of through a picture window that frames a less-than-inviting view.

Choosing one's greenhouse is much like making many other decisions. Start by gathering sufficient information to know what the various choices are. The alternatives might help to enforce your initial impression as to what you believe to be the best kind of greenhouse for your needs or might open entirely new thoughts as to the place your new greenhouse will take in your home and the ways in which you might enjoy it.

The responsibility of a full scale greenhouse might arouse some hesitation, and you may wonder whether you might not be better off with a very small greenhouse to start with. The answer to this is that a smaller one is less expensive and might be easier on your pocketbook. However, it's easier to maintain uniform growing conditions in a larger area than in a small one, so success in growing plants is actually more assured if you gather the initial courage. Even techniques for maintaining plants while you're away are no greater problem in a larger structure.

Starting Small

However, should you decide upon making haste slowly and begin your greenhouse career with a small one, there are window models that are easily installed in single or double windows. They can be heated by the warmth of the room to which they are attached and supplemented in the coldest weather by means of a thermostatically controlled, lead-covered heating cable. In addition to starting and maintaining several house plants an indoor greenhouse will help considerably in growing all your vegetable and bedding planting for the summer garden.

The Attached Greenhouse

The next most convenient, though more expensive, greenhouse is one attached to your home in such a manner that you can enter it without going outdoors. One type is the even-span that is attached to the house at one end with its symmetrical sides gathering most of the available light. By attaching it, you benefit not only by its convenience but by the economy of the utilities being close at hand. If the greenhouse is long enough (25 feet or more) it can be divided into two sections, with the one farthest from the house maintained at a lower temperature. In this way you can satisfy that craving for some of the more exotic subtropical plant species along with a collection of those plants of the temperate regions.

If you use a sliding door to separate the two sections it will take up less room and make it more convenient to leave open during the summer, when the variation between the two artificial climates is least.

Standing on Its Own

The freestanding greenhouse has, built into it, the theoretically perfect conditions. Not being dependent upon the configuration of your home, it can be located anywhere on your property that has the best drainage, most protection from the wind and the maximum amount of daily sunlight. In exchange for these choices it might become necessary to pay an additional sum for connecting your greenhouse to a de-

A window greenhouse needs the top ventilators in the summer, while a lead-coated heating cable is useful during the few cold winter months.

Attaching one end of an even-span greenhouse and finishing off the foundation wall to match the residence provide a unified appearance.

pendable supply of water, electricity and whatever other utilities might be necessary—gas or oil in the case of heating units. The freestanding model also provides an extra degree of flexibility, permitting the easy construction of additional sections to either end at any future date.

The curved-eave greenhouse used to be available only in the most expensive models and was more commonly seen in public conservatories or the orangeries of vast estates. Today, this pleasant subtlety can be incorporated into the smallest greenhouse when the softer line is dictated by the architecture with which it must blend.

When getting into the construction details of the freestanding greenhouse it is so easy to get wrapped up in the minutiae pertaining to the greenhouse proper that one or two other matters may be overlooked. When connecting your electric lines, be certain that the switch can be operated from your house as well as the greenhouse. Put up a floodlight, attached to a tree, if possible, to light your way on dark nights. Also, when digging the trench for water, electric and fuel lines, drop in an extra 1-inch plastic pipe with two pieces of bell wire inside. This additional $15.00 investment (per 100 feet) will enable you to pull through larger electric lines when necessary without additional digging and, in the interim, the bell wire can be hooked up to a comforting alarm system.

The Popular Lean-to

The most popular of all home greenhouses is the lean-to. Having one long wall in common with the house, its remaining side usually leaves sufficient space for plant benches with a

A freestanding model should be tied into the overall landscape plan and, of course, be within easy access of all utilities.

door at one or both ends. A lean-to can be set up against a living room wall so that a window frames a colorful, softly lit scene for evening viewing. An additional door into the greenhouse makes for still greater convenience.

Greenhouses for specialized use have their own special charm such as the "alpine house," which captures the maximum amount of light and, being built into the earth gains an extra amount of insulation. Since the walkway is lower than usual, headroom can also be proportionately less.

The bonus that comes with the lean-to is the luxury of having your greenhouse literally become part of your living area. Whether it is a window greenhouse (a lean-to in miniature) or an entire wall, it can be partitioned off with doors or left open to the rest of the house. Which course of action will be determined by the temperature and degree of humidity you

A footing and low walls must be built to provide solidity even in harshest weather and, at the same time, should be as attractive as possible.

The alpine greenhouse needs to present the glass surface to the sun at an angle as close to perpendicular as possible. The plant benches should be close to the glass.

wish to maintain.

In each step toward deciding which model greenhouse you will buy, there will be a variety of choices—some aesthetic, some mechanical, and, in each case, it will be easier to decide if you have some idea of the kinds of plants you will want to grow. Each range of temperatures carries with it certain limitations and special needs, all of which must be recognized and dealt with—not a difficult task, but one calling for a degree of forethought. Therein lies the source of many greenhouse gardening pleasures.

The lean-to that literally becomes part of the living room is no longer an ordinary greenhouse.

The effect of plants upon the interior of a house cannot be overestimated. Even a small, window greenhouse gives a room a very special quality.

When the proper moisture-resistant materials are used in both furnishings and constructions, the indoor garden becomes practical as well as a pleasure.

3
Selecting the Best Location

In most cases the placement of a greenhouse is almost automatic in that we usually have a preconceived notion as to where such a structure would be most useful, attractive, and least in the way of other activities and views. Even where the decision seems preordained, a confirmation of the factors on the following check list would be useful:

1. Available light. The more light your greenhouse receives each day the more success you will have with a wider selection of plants.

2. The direction and force of the prevailing winds. Moderate air movement provides helpful ventilation, but a constant chilling wind will be reflected in higher heating costs.

3. Surface and subsurface drainage. A foundation seems to ride the constant heaving and settling when excessive water freezes and thaws underground.

4. Convenience. This is paramount, since a greenhouse that is ideal in all other aspects is of little pleasure if its location is not practical.

Naturally, the site that provides the ideal conditions should always be sought; however, it might be of some comfort to know that such a utopian situation is seldom found. Actually, it is the peculiar way in which a greenhouse is made to adjust to its less-than-perfect setting that often gives rise to its special collection of plants, its unique mechanical devices or some other exceptional quality. The plant world is particularly well-suited to helping us resolve these problems. Since there are literally thousands of plant species in every climatic region—cold or warm, high or low, wet or dry, in sun or shade there is no greenhouse that cannot accommodate an interesting group of plants—diverse in all its aspects and eminently satisfying.

Once the site is determined, a little creative foresight becomes necessary in order to develop the greenhouse into the visual asset it should be. The setting immediately surrounding it should be developed either with plants having a softening effect or by creating an integrated development of all those activities related to the greenhouse. They might include a cold frame, cutting and vegetable garden, lath house and an orderly arrangement for soil, compost, potsherds, etc.

Fitting It to Your Property

As greenhouse gardeners we all-too often become so engrossed in the activities of cultivating plants that the visual effect of our surroundings might escape us entirely. Since the area is viewed just as often from the outside as it is from within consider both aspects and utilize whatever plants are appropriate in shielding, accenting or softening your greenhouse structure. Examine the setting critically—both day and night, from whatever position it will normally be seen. If the bench is to be filled with attractive, colorful, flowering plants and they would be obscured as soon as you are seated in the living room, a second thought would seem proper in repositioning the height of the wall.

It is a never-ending source of surprise to find how fearful and inadequate people feel when faced with the first major decisions of con-

Considering a greenhouse from only one vantage point can result in overlooking other features. Look at the greenhouse from both outdoors and in—and utilize it accordingly.

With its own potting shed and cold frames, this greenhouse is a self-sufficient plant growing center.

structing a greenhouse. Its position on the property seems to be one of those decisions which induces traumas so, before reading further, *please* rid yourself of the mistaken notion that some sort of special talent is necessary for success. What *is* necessary is a logical approach to the subject, a realistic appraisal of the patterns of your everyday life and thoughtful consideration of your horticultural aspirations. A propagation greenhouse is certainly not as colorful a sight to look out upon as is a display house of flowering pot plants so the subject of use logically becomes an important factor in deciding upon the location of your greenhouse. The propagation house would fit into the business-like atmosphere off the kitchen while the display of flowering plants is more in tune with the aesthetics of the living room and could be linked to it through a picture window or sliding glass doors, thereby enhancing both the house and the greenhouse. Even a freestanding greenhouse can be linked by a path, planting, or portico without actually being connected. Add some soft nonglare interior night lighting and you soon complete a picture that makes the site seem like it was the only logical one, right from the start.

Bear in mind that it's often easier and less expensive to work within one's existing conditions than to try changing them. It might mean putting it on a second floor porch—but why not? What rule says that a greenhouse must be in any set traditional location? A site chosen by good sense, instead of by arbitrary rules that don't fit your specific case or needs, will most often result in a gratifying greenhouse. While a minimum of three hours of good sunlight is necessary each day for most flowering plants a deficiency can be corrected with a few well-placed fluorescent fixtures.

Now that you are feeling completely relaxed and satisfied with your decision you will find no difficulty in facing and dealing with the more mechanical aspects of adapting your newly chosen site to your greenhouse so that its maximum potential may be achieved with a minimum of site-related problems.

Coping with the Elements

If lack of sufficient light is a result of a fixed object such as a house or steep hillside, of course the forementioned fluorescent fixtures will do wonders toward building the light level to that approaching normalcy. If a tree is the source of your problem it can be judiciously pruned so that its appearance does not suffer but the amount of light improves. Do not try to change the natural environment too drastically. Better still, after upgrading the light somewhat, work with what you have. The thousands of plant species that thrive on the jungle floor in the Amazon Valley probably enjoy less light than you are able to supply.

Now take a look at the exposure from the standpoint of wind. An occasional windy day is of little consequence; however, if there seems to exist a daily diet of cold winds of rather constant high velocity, some measures must be taken to minimize the problem. It is not only the extra heating cost that is of concern but the chilling effect is detrimental to steady plant growth. Fortunately, from both a cost and aesthetic standpoint a solid barrier is *not* the answer. Wind only increases its force after passing over a wall—much the way a roller coaster builds up speed upon reaching a crest. Stiff breezes are effectively slowed down when broken up by an obstacle of open construction or form. A lattice, a deciduous hedge or a few strategically placed shrubs will do nicely.

Sometimes an unlikely location proves to be extra special. An area right off the bedroom can make for a pleasant solarium–sitting room–plant room combination.

A self-contained gardening area, with the greenhouse, cold frames, and potting shed placed in a convenient, sunny location.

Prune for additional light when overshadowed by trees.

Any water added to the greenhouse environment must be controllable. This is done easily in the case of water which *you* add to the soil or in humidifying the atmosphere. However, ground water which is a result of the slope of the surrounding land or the character of the subsoil also should be controlled. Drainage tiles or perforated pipe can be installed to carry off excess water, thereby alleviating the greenhouse foundation from possible winter damage through heaving due to freezing.

Having improved upon your natural surroundings, you are now ready to prepare your greenhouse further toward creating an artificial environment.

Open hedges or fences will break the force of prevailing winds, keep fuel bills down and plant quality up.

Areas improperly drained can cause havoc in greenhouse foundations and create perpetual dampness — a haven for fungus diseases. Install perforated drain tiles to disperse excess water downhill.

A chosen site can be ideal as a sun pocket, but it must have good ventilation. Test flow of air on several days using a metal can filled with smoldering paper.

4
How to Build Different Kinds of Greenhouses

Since no one type of greenhouse is the "only one" that is perfect for any given situation *you* automatically become the expert who can decide which you would like. While one might have some minor drawbacks such as the lean-to not having quite as much bench space as an equivalent size freestanding model, it *does* have a wall upon which many interesting vines can be grown, fruits can be espaliered and tiers of shelves can be arranged. Weighing the loss of one against the luxury of the other might seem like a difficult choice, but the nice thing is that neither decision can be *wrong*. Only the bonuses differ.

Below Ground

Now you are ready to erect your new greenhouse. The manufacturer will supply you with simple plans as soon as you place your order so that you can start constructing the foundation and have it completed as soon as the greenhouse components arrive. The climate in your area will determine just what kind of foundation is necessary. Where the weather is mild and above freezing the year round only a footing will be needed. A row or two of cement blocks will provide you with a level surface for attaching the greenhouse parts. Where more severe climate is the rule, a deeper trench, with additional concrete blocks, from the surface to the maximum depth to which your ground freezes will be necessary. This will prevent heaving and settling which would create an unlevel condition and eventually cause glass to break and joints to become drafty.

Above Ground

You can now set your greenhouse directly upon the foundation or build a wall about 3 feet above ground level. The former method provides a glass-to-ground greenhouse which allows the maximum amount of light to enter the greenhouse under the benches and, in the absence of benches, permits you to plant directly in the ground for such tall plants as tomatoes, sweet peas, etc. The use of a wall is usually preferred—especially in colder, northern areas in order to conserve on heat. The lowest few feet are usually several degrees cooler than conventional bench height—a further reason for deciding to use an above-ground wall construction. It is usually at this point of attaching the greenhouse to the foundation that the mason leaves, and you or a contractor take over. The mason usually will have inserted bolts (according to the plans) in the cement joints of the foundation wall, leaving a few inches of the threaded portion protruding so that the rigid greenhouse members can be firmly attached.

While most home greenhouses *can* be erected by a reasonably competent "do-it-yourselfer," the luxury of having a professional do the job will insure its completion within a few days with a minimum amount of aggravation. Such details as lead anchors for attaching bolts into brick walls are standard supplies for the contractor but mean an extra trip to the busy hardware store on Saturday afternoon for the amateur.

The foundation walls not only provide helpful insulation but form a smooth union of the greenhouse with the adjacent house by using an appropriate facing material. The wooden greenhouse has been considered the workhorse in both commercial and residential installations for a century or more. Wood has great insulation powers and it even absorbs heat radiated by the sun during the day and slowly releases it during the night. Of course wood also has the advantage inside the greenhouse of making it easy to attach a variety of shelving, lights, brackets, and even hanging plants.

The Superstructure

In spite of all these advantages, plus the initial low cost of construction, wood can no longer keep up with the tremendous advantages built up in recent years by aluminum. The nearly-no-upkeep has, in itself, made aluminum the first choice almost every time. Even the change of an accidentally broken pane of glass is a

First, check with local officials to see if a construction permit is necessary. It may be necessary to reconcile prefab with present structure by attaching a frame on which to add greenhouse sections.

Walls and floor must be made level.

simple no-putty operation involving glass, a few screws and pieces of plastic weatherstripping. Proof of the acceptance of aluminum for use by the amateur is the fact that the corner hardware store now stocks self-threading metal screws—formerly only found in sheet metal shops. The writer has maintained one wooden greenhouse and one made of aluminum for more than twenty-five years. The wooden one has been painted every year or two to keep the wood from rotting and the caulking has been replaced twice on all the glass. The aluminum greenhouse has never required maintenance of any kind to its structure—not even replacing a broken pane of glass.

If you have decided upon having a collection of tropical plants the atmosphere will of course need to carry a high percentage of humidity. Should your greenhouse be a lean-to it would be wise to take special precautions to protect the wall of the house against which it rests. Any openings should be well caulked and the surface should be given two coats of good exterior paint. The constant humidity will not affect a wooden greenhouse for many years since the greenhouse will have been made of redwood or cypress, but the outside wall of your house was not made to endure a constantly humid atmosphere.

Before you enclose the outside walls, at least preliminary preparation of the soil would be helpful. Remove all the rubble and the top 12 inches of compacted soil. This should be replaced later with a friable soil mixture of the proper makeup to support the growth of the plants you will be growing. Several wheelbarrow loads of gravel should be on hand to prepare the bedding for walkways. Ordering such materials as gravel at the same time as the sand and cement blocks will save a second delivery charge and you will need it within a week or two of the completion of the foundation. If your foundation is shallow due to your mild local climate, you would do well to lay

Roof panels will then fit with no problem.

The structure can be completed in one full, but satisfying, day.

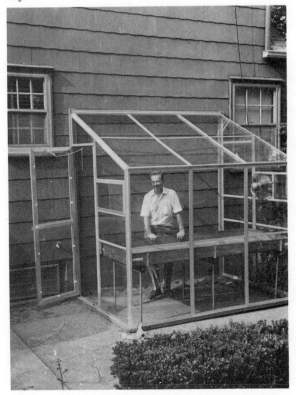

down a piece of hardware cloth (heavy-mesh galvanized screening) from wall to wall, at the level of the lowest concrete block. This barrier will discourage burrowing rodents, that will be attracted by the wonderful new supply of delicacies to add to their winter diet.

Research continues at most land-grant colleges into the design of greenhouses for both private and commercial use. It is often the importance of a particular industry such as tomato or carnation growing that helps develop methods that the home gardener capitalizes upon and adapts to his needs.

New Developments Continue

Only a few years ago sheet plastics disintegrated in sunlight and the rigid ones fogged up, but newly developed materials now provide a highly satisfactory level of light with a minimum of support structure necessary and therefore very little shadow to adversely affect plant growth. Many land-grant colleges will supply complete construction plans for a practical, inexpensive greenhouse clad in plastic. The fee of approximately ten dollars certainly represents good value.

With the explosion of leisure industries greenhouses and their potential owners have benefited considerably. While inflation has adversely affected many products, greenhouses of newer and more diverse designs may be purchased today, made of more interesting materials at lower prices than ever before. It is true that the expensive ones are perhaps more expensive than ever but the alternatives are even more attractive.

In contacting land-grant colleges (the Department of Ornamental Horticulture) select those which are in areas having a climate similar to your own, since their efforts will be primarily for home consumption. The state universities in Ohio, Illinois, Pennsylvania, New York, California and Oregon, to name a few, have done interesting work in this area of study.

The experimental models developed by the land-grant colleges are usually inexpensive and practical. The material used as covering is under constant evaluation and their latest recommendation is usually readily available.

Even seasonal greenhouses such as this one have their place in the suburbs. Popular Science can provide more information on this particular geodesic model.

Considerable effort is made to design private greenhouses so that they are aesthetically pleasing. Another important factor in northern areas is their snow load resistance. But, whatever the use or wherever the location the overriding attention must be given to one critical element: the angle at which the sun's rays hit the glass. Light hitting the glass at a perpendicular angle will pass directly through with greater intensity and less refraction than light hitting the glass at an angle closer to the parallel. At a right angle, less of the light spectrum will be lost.

The materials used for walks within your greenhouse are important. Their appearance is but one factor and is subject to individual preference. Comfort is another consideration. Wood, having a degree of resilience is good if you will be standing for long periods of time. Gravel also has its benefits. High humidity and high temperatures often mean mosses and algae will make the walks slippery so a coarse or rough surface would be preferable in this case. If slatted walks are to be used, make them easily removable so that they can be scrubbed outdoors and the area under them can be sprayed with an insecticide periodically.

In propagating greenhouses, the headroom is of least importance since most plants grown are in their earliest and smallest stages. Only the gardener's headroom need be considered and this can be accomplished by recessing the walk a few feet below the surface. Heat can be introduced below the benches, where the additional warmth will do the most good.

A coarse brick floor with sand joints can help maintain a bit of moisture in the atmosphere.

Wooden slats are easy on the legs in the work area.

If there is any secret to building a good foundation, it is constant checking to make sure walls are straight and level. Each error at ground level becomes magnified as the height increases.

Fieldstone walls can fit an otherwise foreign structure into the setting in a most natural way.

Double wood walls can be insulated with fiberglass to provide good protection against a severe climate. They will also harmonize with the surrounding architecture.

5
How to Create
the Proper Climate

While flowers usually create the show expected of them in the wild, the rest of the plant often does not pass close examination. Just take a walk through the woods—almost anywhere—and see the percentage of trees fallen, leaning, or just barely surviving. On the other hand many plants will never achieve their full potential grown in a flower pot but this limitation is confined only to the element of size. Insofar as all other aspects of plant growth, (vigor, color of foliage and flowering) be assured that you can not merely approach nature's successes but even surpass them. When you consider your ability to protect plants from the debilitating effects of all of nature's catastrophes in the artificial but ideal climate of the greenhouse, it is little wonder that such grand, ego-inflating results are possible.

Control of Light

Once you decide just which kind of climate you wish to emulate (tropical, temperate, alpine or any other specific kind of environment) you will then be ready to reproduce all its elements—light, heat, air and water. Of the four elements involved, light is the one of which you will be most keenly aware since your own mood is often affected by cheerfully bright days or gloomy overcast ones. While plants express no feelings (in spite of those who will vehemently disagree on this point) their performance will be closely linked to the weather and, in particular, the amount of light which is available each day. It is easier to control excess light than to compensate for a marginal or inadequate supply. The control of light can be accomplished in a number of ways but all methods should be applied to the outside of the greenhouse. Once light is allowed to penetrate the glass and enter the greenhouse the heat will also have entered and must then be expelled. It is much easier to avoid excessive heat in the first place. While the application of a semi-permanent shading compound (whitewash plus kerosene in a mixture of 3 to 1) is unadjustable to the weather conditions, it is the least expensive method of controlling unwanted light. Roller blinds made of wood slats are wonderfully adjustable but are becoming quite expensive. Shades made of plastic netting are an excellent substitute. In dealing with light you will be able to tell by feel that its intensity affects the heat and humidity. As light entering the greenhouse increases in its intensity the temperature also rises. This, in turn, will dry up the humidity in the atmosphere, so you can see that an appreciation of each of these elements

The sunny side is protected from burning sun with green
plastic sheets fitted onto the inside surface of the glass.
When warmth becomes excessive, the exhaust fan pushes out
the hot air and pulls in cooler air from vents near ground
level.

Wooden roller blinds are worth their high price. They can be adjusted to meet the demands of the
weather.

Any system such as this plastic screening that prevents the warmth from reaching the glass surface will improve the greenhouse environment during the summer months. The metal and wire frame holds the screening at least 6 inches from the glass.

At the height of summer sun, whitewash can be applied to keep the interior from overheating. As the summer wanes, the shading compound can be partially removed with a putty knife. By removing more whitewash every few weeks, additional light can enter, until the glass is completely clean in November.

and some knowledge of how to control them are valuable assets in mastering the greenhouse environment.

Adding Warmth— Where Necessary

If you live where a touch of frost is not unusual then you will also need to warm your greenhouse during the winter months. The method you choose should be the most dependable, least expensive and feasible in terms of space. Each system (gas, oil or electric) can heat water in a radiator or can work in conjunction with a blower to circulate warm air throughout the greenhouse. Radiators will provide the most even temperature, though warm air blowers will be slightly less troublesome. However, the latter needs supplementary humidification since the movement of warm air has a drying effect on the atmosphere.

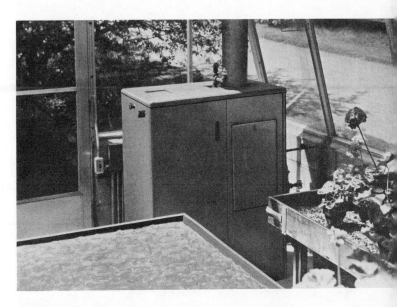

Systems for heating hot water are made extremely compact and use either oil or gas.

In large areas, the fan blowing across water pipes will move the warmed air quickly but gently.

The speed with which fin-tube radiators can heat the air is impressive. The extra amount of surface presented to the air accounts for their efficiency.

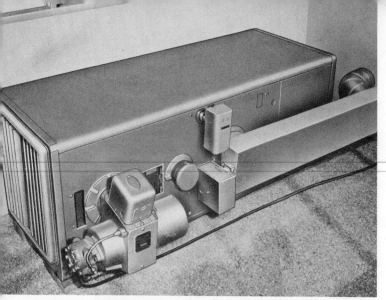

Well-insulated, compact oil burners will send warm air on demand of the thermostat, at relatively low cost.

Gas heaters are now made so that all noxious fumes are expelled outdoors and they can be installed under the greenhouse bench, through the foundation wall.

The installation of a heating system is often the largest investment after the greenhouse itself, so it is particularly important that its selection and installation are up to professional standards. A cool greenhouse calls for the maintenance of a minimum nighttime temperature of 45 to 50°F. and an ideal maximum of 55°F. during the day. The intermediate greenhouse should get no colder than 50 to 55°F. at night and is best kept at about 65°F. during the day. The warm greenhouse is run at 60 to 70°F. at night and can be above 80°F. during the day. In order to achieve these limits, a plumbing concern can match the cubic dimensions to be heated with the proper size burner. All heating devices are rated in terms of British Thermal Units, and although this engineering parlance might be foreign, any competent plumber or electrician can give you the magic figure in BTU's so you can shop for the right size unit regardless of what form of power it uses to generate heat or the form in which the heat is delivered.

Clear the Air

Air, the third element in the quartet of essential factors, must be in supply all the time. Not so little as to create a stuffy atmosphere nor so much as to create drafts. Of course, there is a scientific formula related to the number of times per hour that an entirely new supply of air is exchanged within the greenhouse, but in order to avoid such precise measurements we suggest that the proper atmosphere be one you can actually feel on your face upon entering the greenhouse. One that is overly moist or one that is drafty and cool is easily detected and the proper adjustment can be made—little by little—until it feels correct for the climate you are trying to emulate.

All automatic equipment becomes automatic only after it has been regulated to react at a given point. Having arrived at this point and set the equipment, it must be monitored occasionally. Even the most sophisticated computer will provide correct answers only after it is properly programmed by a live, thinking person and still requires periodic inspection. Since automatic ventilators are activated by thermostatic changes, it is essential that the control box is shielded from the sun so that it re-

Electric heaters are fine where small areas are to be kept at warm temperature levels.

The manually-operated ventilators are more of a luxury than the automatic ones since they require someone on duty all the time to react to the weather.

This ingenious nonelectric automatic ventilator is magically activated when fluid expanding with the heat pushes the arm outward in a hydraulic action.

Set up to predetermined limits, the electrically-operated ventilator will keep the greenhouse climate in control. The device on the right is set to activate the heaters when needed.

The successor to the electric fan, this air turbulator will move the air without draftiness.

The evaporative cooler is a most efficient method of cooling the greenhouse atmosphere.

cords the temperature of the greenhouse in the broadest sense rather than recording the heat of the sun focused directly upon the metal box containing the mechanism.

Up to now we have been concerned primarily with the introduction of air both to provide oxygen and to regulate the buildup of high temperatures. Now, if we take the need for air one step further, we will see that during the summer, in some locations, the mere opening of a ventilator is not sufficient to bring the fresh air into all parts of the greenhouse. Such still air must be coaxed a bit and, to do this properly, a turbulator is useful. This first cousin to the electric fan has the ability to move the air without creating a draft. The shape of the blades is such that it breaks up the flow of air and sends it off in different directions in bits and pieces.

Controlling the Moisture

The turbulator does well until you try to do the same job at still hotter times of the year. When the outside temperature reaches 85 to 100°F. and you are trying to grow carnations, alpine plants or those orchids from the cooler regions of the world it becomes extremely difficult to maintain the proper growing conditions without some means of cooling the greenhouse air. An expensive air conditioner is unnecessary, but a more reasonably priced and simply operated evaporative cooler can work wonders. This is basically a box situated next to and outside of the greenhouse. It takes warm air from outside, passes it through a moistened filter, then circulates the cool air into the greenhouse by means of a fan in the rear of the box. The air, cooled by the water, can lower the greenhouse temperature by as much as 25° on a hot day. However, the air will not be dehumidified at this time when the high moisture content is needed. When we speak of water, moisture or humidity in the context of greenhouse gardening, all three forms of moisture may exist in the air, the soil, or within the plants. If the atmosphere remains buoyant, then there is little change in the soil moisture or that drawn out of the plants themselves. However, if the temperature rises to the point where it begins to dry out the atmosphere, it will be essential to replace the moisture quickly. The best way (and the most painless) to maintain the proper humidity is with a humidifier hooked up to a humidistat. Then, your ventilators are set to open and close at predetermined levels. Add to this the thermostat that regulates your heat and then decide upon your shading method. After a few weeks of juggling these four elements that make up your artificial climate, you will have developed a measure of control that will improve continuously.

When the water is turned on, the small hole in the lead weight allows a drop at a time to continue flowing until the soil is completely saturated. The duration of each watering can be regulated automatically.

Groups of plants with similar needs can be provided with optimum humidity with a portable humidifier.

One of today's systems for simplifying watering chores uses spaghetti-like tubes, each leading from a main water hose to an individual pot.

A humidifier attached to a water source and having a large fan will break up water droplets and disperse them throughout the greenhouse to the degree called for by a pre-set humidistat.

6
All about Workspace and Display

As your greenhouse goes up there is bound to be a certain amount of fantasizing but, by the time you are ready to furnish its interior you will have come down to earth and be ready to settle upon a useful and attractive arrangement. But whatever it is, construct and attach things so they can be moved without too much trouble. One of the great pleasures of greenhouse gardening is the almost magical ease with which you can switch from a tropical habitat to a desert environment whenever a whim dictates.

It would be helpful to bear in mind the inventory of elements with which you may work to perform these miraculous changes: Walls, walks, ground beds, benches, shelves, brackets and hooks for hanging plants, trellises, and training wires. Variations of each of these, worked into a scheme, can produce an efficient use of space, an ideal method of growing specific plants and a comfortable area in which to garden the year round. Remember, while the greenhouse structure itself is often one taken out of inventory from the manufacturer's warehouse, the handling of its interior can and should be completely individualized for your needs. If you are left-handed, do not settle for a door knob on the wrong side. If you are six feet three, do not spend your leisure time hunched over a plant bench three feet high.

Use of Space

The conventional arrangement for a freestanding greenhouse calls for plant benches with one or two walkways. If the greenhouse width is a minimum of 15 feet, two plant benches can be situated along the two long walls running the length of the greenhouse with another in the center, having a walk along each side. A lean-to most often has one ell-shaped bench along the long wall away from the house and one short wall. Whatever the bench arrangement, choose the material and size suited to your needs. If you will be growing most of your plants in pots, redwood will prove superior. The wood itself will hold some moisture as well as absorb warmth. Both will be released slowly to the benefit of the growing environment. Wood benches need not be merely one large flat surface when a grandstand arrangement will show off your flowering plants to greater advantage and enjoyment. The tiered row of steps should face south so they benefit from the maximum amount of sunlight and cast no shade upon other plants. If, however, the entire bench is to be filled with soil and the plants grown in the bench rather than in pots, it is preferable to build the benches out of transite, a cement product sold in sheets at most building supply yards. A well-arranged greenhouse will utilize shelves for pot plants, slabs of tree fern to support epiphytes and even hooks to suspend those plants with a trailing habit.* Even in the under-bench areas ground-cover plants can be grown and some can be trained upon the bench legs to soften the hard look of metal parts. The luxury of a potting shed cannot always be worked into a green-house plan; however, close quarters often pro-vide the most ingenious, handiest and most or-derly use of space. Just look at the galley on any 25- or 30-foot boat for proof. If a room is close by with enough heat for comfort while working, build a few shelves for supplies, a cupboard for sprays and other chemicals; make room for a few plastic containers of garbage-can size to store leaf mold, sand and soil. Leave table top space at a comfortable height to do your transplanting and other chores. When finished, it will be a potting shed, even if in reality it is a corner of the garage or part of the laundry room in the basement.

*Entire walls as well as partitions make excellent sup-ports for flowering vines.

Arranging tiers of pot plants as a grandstand will make greater use of an area without diminishing the amount of light and ventilation available to each plant.

For pot plants it's hard to improve upon redwood benches for both durability and holding a helpful degree of humidity.

When growing plants directly in a soil-filled bench, a prefabricated cement product called transite will resist rotting and prove useful for many years.

When air circulation is essential, a heavy wire mesh called hardware cloth is ideal. It also provides good water drainage and cuts down on the places insects can hide and multiply. Orchids do particularly well on this type of bench.

A potting shed, of course, is a wonderful place to extend one's greenhouse activities. Handy storage of soils, chemicals, tools, and pots makes potting, grooming, propagating, and pruning that much simpler.

A well-located work area — everything within easy reach — is sometimes little more than using the only space that's available.

Glass shelving takes care of seasonal crowding without seriously affecting the amount of light.

A lean-to greenhouse is often ideal for orchids — here grown on slabs of tree fern and hung onto sheets of wire mesh. But any plant can be hung on a blank wall to catch the full sun and utilize the space above bench height.

Few plant displays are more attractive than the hanging basket. Given the necessary feeding and watering, these plants will fill out and flower profusely as they benefit from the ample light and ventilation.

A number of vines are effective in softening architectural elements such as partitions and doorways. This nasturtium is effective for eight or nine months out of the year but a jasmine or allamanda can satisfy the need all year around.

A lath structure for "summering" plants makes an attractive adjunct to the greenhouse.

A lath-roofed shelter can easily be attached to the potting shed.

A cold frame is a valuable aid in hardening off all those seedlings and cuttings, started in the greenhouse, prior to planting them in the outdoor garden. This one is a light-weight portable model, though ones of permanent redwood can easily be built.

Why Not Have a
Tropical Sitting Room?

With a bit of planning, the mundane necessities of day-to-day plant care can be hidden and only lush growth will surround your chairs and table. A perfect place to read the Sunday paper.

The plant benches were removed from the greenhouse pictured on the right and with a little spade work, a bucket or two of waterproof cement and wire reinforcement, a shallow pool was completed in an hour or two. Add a number of stones to form a natural looking course for the water. Place a small electric submersible pump in a sump about 14 inches deep and position just under the waterfall so that the turbulence will hide its existence. A selection of ferns, creeping plants and a few others chosen for their attractive foliage can be placed either directly in the ground, where possible, or in shallow pots and trained on the rubber tube at the top of the water course. Place your furniture, plug in the water pump and presto—a tropical setting with the feel, smell and sound of the real thing!

You don't even have to be a mason to set wire form in a roughly dug excavation.

Waterproof cement is easily mixed and poured.

Then, with a few well-chosen rocks, a variety of moisture loving plants at poolside, a small recirculating water pump, and one or two pieces of furniture, you have a tropical sitting room for your daily "trip south."

7
Tools and Supplies

Greenhouse tools that can be categorized as essential are relatively few but those few should be of the best quality you can afford. Though rubber hose is more expensive and heavier in weight than plastic, it is always supple and a pleasure to use. A carbon steel knife can easily be kept razor sharp while stainless steel seldom has a keen edge even though it is rust resistant. On the other hand, a stainless steel trowel is hard to beat. Its smooth surface cleans thoroughly and does its job easily, and so it is with many tools which have changed very little in design in the past century. The English and German watering cans are perfect examples of a hard-to-improve traditional design. But any gardener worth the name will be on the lookout constantly for ingenious new methods of doing the many greenhouse chores. New products are always coming out and some are very inventive and do a specific job superbly. The tensiometer is one that did not exist at a practical level until a few years ago. Now the greenhouse gardener can determine accurately and almost instantaneously whether or not a pot needs watering.

Good equipment will not make a good gardener but it will make you a better gardener and will eliminate many potential frustrations.

When there are so many interrelated elements as is the case in growing plants in an artificial environment, it is perhaps impossible to label any one as "the most important." However, taking the liberty to be dogmatic, I believe watering is that "all-important" facet. Too little water pulls you into the false satisfaction that all is well, when actually, the plant is slowly dying. Excessive water can produce the same disastrous results by smothering the roots, which will then rot. It therefore becomes essential to learn how much watering is "just right." It is here that the right tools make the job easier. First, an inexpensive tensiometer will tell you about the existing condition and, if you have read a little about each of your plants, you will know whether it thrives under conditions that are dry, moist or moderate. In order to apply water liberally and yet not wash away the soil, a water breaker will be most useful. It is a simple hose attachment that cuts the force of the stream of water. For still lighter applications, misting is beneficial. The plants will lose less water if their surfaces and the greenhouse benches and walks are misted occasionally.

The Right Tool for Each Job
The Best You Can Afford

For Daily Care:

Plastic garbage cans for storage
of soil components

Split bamboo stakes

Soft twine for staking

Portable trombone sprayer
for insecticides and fungicides

Galvanized pail

Scissor-type pruning shears

A mister is attached to the hose nozzle for gentle spraying or for cooling plants without soaking them.

A well-balanced watering can is the easiest to control. The flow of water is regulated by using the "rose" on the spout for seedlings and young plants or detaching the rose where heavier waterings are needed.

The force of the stream of water is reduced by using a water breaker on the nozzle.

Establish a handy, yet out-of-the-way, storage place for hose when not in use.

Tensiometers are available in many forms to help you determine whether or not your plants need water.

For Greenhouse Maintenance:

1 long-handled broom for floor

1 short-handled broom
for tables and benches

1 dust pan

3-foot step ladder

Hammer and assorted nails

Screwdriver and assorted screws

Paint brush and scraper
for shading compounds

For Watering:

Rubber hose
(only as long as
absolutely necessary)

Nozzles for misting, fogging, spraying

Couplers at faucet and between hoses

Watering can (no larger than you can
lift comfortably when filled)

Wooden-soled shoes or clogs
(warm in winter and feet stay dry)

Plant labels, color coded to warn
against watering dormant plants

For Planting:

Stainless steel trowel

Scoop for soil, sand, etc.

Scissors for cutting screen, string
and trimming roots, etc.

Coarse and fine strainers

Dibble, even a heavy knitting needle,
for poking planting holes in the soil

*A few simple tools, galvanized wire, and a series of bends
and . . .*

*A quick-coupler at each hose location is a real blessing for
speeding up watering chores.*

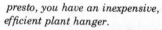

*A water mixer is invaluable in taking the excessive chill out
of water in midwinter.*

*presto, you have an inexpensive,
efficient plant hanger.*

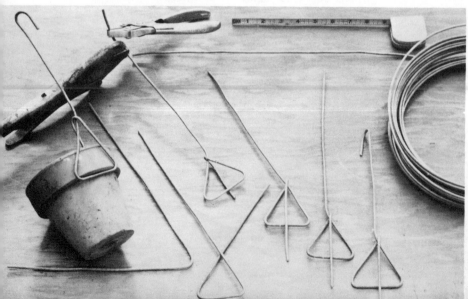

For Transplanting:

Trowel

Dibble for marking holes for seedlings

Sieves in three degrees of fineness

Tin snips for cutting wire and screening

Scoop for mixing soil, sand,
    peat moss, etc.

For Propagation:

A sharp knife and a carborundum stone
    and oil to keep it sharp

Scrub brush and pail for disinfecting
    propagation container before
    each use

Plastic bags and twistems
    for air layering

For Plant Maintenance:

Lightweight, small volume
    insecticide sprayer

Soft twine

Pruning shears of scissor-action type

Tack gun for attaching
    plastic sheeting

Plastic pail, approximately 3 gallons

Bamboo stakes

There are a variety of portable heaters for emergency use, and one might save your plants in a winter power failure.

A battery-operated temperature alarm is an excellent early warning device.

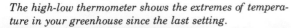

The high-low thermometer shows the extremes of temperature in your greenhouse since the last setting.

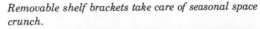

Removable shelf brackets take care of seasonal space crunch.

8
What You Should Know about Potting and Planting

Many plant ills stem from the confined conditions in which they are grown within their containers and, until you understand how to work with either natural or artificial materials in creating good drainage, soil texture, and fertilizer mixtures, success cannot be assured. Even the proportion of the root mass to the size of the container is critical in maintaining the proper degree of soil moisture without forcing out the oxygen, which is equally essential. Handling plants in these early stages of growth is doubly important in that their resistance to insect attack and disease is significantly improved when growth is most efficient and vigorous.

The first potting should take place after a seedling has acquired its second set of true leaves. The first leaves are often round, smooth edged and unlike the typical leaves which are produced subsequently. By this time, the food in the seed itself will have been consumed and a more nutritious medium will be necessary. There are a number of choices of containers and many offer greater convenience rather than any great improvement in growth potential. The least expensive is the wooden or papier-mâché flat (shallow box approximately 14 x 18 x 2 inches) in which seedlings can be spaced about 2 inches apart and when ready for the next move, either into the garden or into an individual pot, each plant can be cut apart from the next with a knife as a cake is cut into squares before coming out of the baking pan.

Clay Pots vs. Plastic

The choice of the individual pot is of far greater importance than one would suspect. Each kind of container has its own limitations and reactions; therefore it would be helpful to understand the important differences of each. I happen to favor the clay pot because it always seems to tell me something. When dry it is lighter in color; when there are excesses of lime in the water or salts in the soil, a white coating will build up on the outside of the pot. If drainage is insufficient, the pot itself will dispel some of the excess through its porous walls.

There are, however, champions of the plastic pot. They are cheaper, lighter and do not have to be watered as often. Since they evaporate water more slowly than clay, do not position the two kinds together. They cannot be handled on an equal basis.

The molded pots are new and wonderful for plants in their early stages. Some are made of peat moss and others of paper. They usually contain a small

Too little soil (left) and too much (right) prevent proper water retention. Correct size (center) also provides correct space for optimum root growth.

The right size and shape pots will help your plants achieve successful growth.

amount of fertilizer within their walls which helps young plants to get started. Be sure that these pots are moistened (damp but not soaking wet) before adding the soil and the plant. If not, water added to the soil subsequently will not be able to penetrate the composition walls of the pot and the roots will be restricted within the pot. The plant will eventually suffer from lack of nutrition and the necessarily small root area will be unable to support any additional top growth. The soil used in the first stages of growth can be of low fertility and a porous texture. However, once its roots and top structure begin to develop, it needs more nutrition and a more specific texture. It is now that we start our efforts to emulate the plant's native growing conditions. An inventory of basic ingredients mixed according to recipe is an orderly way to get each plant started properly.

Watch Your Plants Closely

In potting any plant, it is not only important to know something of the kind of soil in which it thrives but its particular life cycle. For these and other reasons it would be helpful to learn some of the biographical data of each plant, in order to reproduce the best possible growing conditions.

Each plant has a specific period for active growth, flowering and resting. In some plants it is obvious as to which period the plant is passing through, and in others the dormancy is slight. Observation will arm you with this knowledge *after* the fact, but a little simple research will prepare you for what is about to happen in the case of newly acquired plants.

Soil Mixtures

In order to create the various soil compositions a few basic materials are necessary:

Garden topsoil, put through a ½-inch mesh screen

Coarse peat moss

Leaf mold or compost

Coarse sand

Dehydrated cow manure

Bone meal

All-Purpose Mixture	*Highly Porous Mixture*
½ topsoil	⅔ topsoil
¼ peat moss	⅓ coarse sand
¼ coarse sand	

Organic Mixture	*Highly Organic Mixture*
⅓ topsoil	¼ topsoil
⅓ peat moss	⅛ peat moss
⅓ coarse sand	⅛ coarse sand
	½ leaf mold or compost

NOTE: Add to each bushel of the above mixtures 1½ pints (dry measure) of dehydrated cow manure and ½ pint (dry measure) of bone meal.

A soil pasteurizer holding manageable quantities can ready your soil mixture in a few hours.

A pH test is imperative before any corrective measures can be taken in preparing your soil mixtures.

Soils, chemicals, and fertilizers should be stored in a dry location and labeled fully.

Soil-less Potting Mixtures

Soil-less potting mixtures are becoming increasingly popular and, since they eliminate expensive pasturizing equipment, are economical as well as overcoming the threat of a great variety of diseases. Two of the recommended formulas are:

Modified Cornell Mix

½ bushel peat moss

½ bushel horticultural grade vermiculite

or

½ bushel perlite in place of vermiculite

plus

5 tablespoons ground limestone

3 teaspoons superphosphate, 20% powdered

8 teaspoons 5–10–5 fertilizer

Modified California Mix

½ bushel shredded peat moss

½ bushel fine sand

½ teaspoon potassium nitrate

½ teaspoon potassium sulphate

15 teaspoons dolomitic limestone

5 teaspoons agricultural limestone

5 teaspoons superphosphate, 20% powdered

½ teaspoon chelated iron

By varying the basic components, soil mixtures with the proper texture can be prepared.

Before adding rough drainage materials, place screening at bottom of the pot as a barrier against root-chewing insects.

In addition to different sizes there is a variety of shapes and materials — clay, paper, peat, and plastic.

Molded paper cubes hold water easily and individually planted seedlings take hold quickly.

Replanting when root-bound will stimulate flowering and encourage further growth.

Daffodils, tulips, crocus and iris can be crowded when potted with no ill effects.

This first and last watering before forcing should be thorough.

After potting, place in cool location covered with sand or wood shavings to permit root growth before becoming dormant.

When frozen, cover to protect against a possible thaw.

There is something mysterious about growing orchids that draws each new greenhouse owner to try his hand at it. Perhaps it is the tremendous variety (over 5,000 species) not only in size of the flowers (from ⅛ inch to 7 or 8 inches) but in texture, color and perfume. Some are terrestrial, growing in organic soil while others are epiphytes, and are at home growing upon trees though getting their nourishment principally from the air. The latter category needs a special potting medium to which the plant roots can be anchored as well as a unique procedure to anchor them. The potting method is equally specialized.

Pots or flats should be brought into progressively warmer temperatures, given more intense light and increased watering as growth quickens.

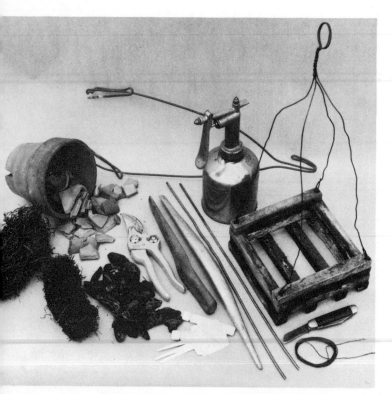

Orchid potting calls for its own special tools — wooden rafts, wire stakes, osmunda fiber, potting stick, charcoal chunks, perforated pots and wire hangers.

When the roots walk out of the pot, an orchid is ready for repotting.

Cut plant apart, with each section having 3 or 4 pseudobulbs and an active eye or bud, and trim the roots.

Stand each section in its own pot, forcing osmunda fiber around the roots, keeping the rhizome close to the surface.

Potted and staked, new plant should be firmly anchored in its container.

9
Keeping Your Plants in Good Health— and Treating Those That Aren't

During a plant's period of active growth it is essential that it be given all the ingredients to maintain good vigor. Whatever it does not receive soon becomes a limiting factor in its progress toward producing seed. In the gardener's world, the goal is having his plants produce a number of attractive flowers, while from nature's standpoint the production of seeds is the desirable end result. In hurrying a plant toward *its* goal, be sure that you don't wear it out prematurely. Both annuals and biennials will continue flowering for many weeks in their effort to produce seeds, if their flowers are cut after they open fully. If allowed to go to seed immediately they will have completed their growth cycle and therefore will stop flowering. In the case of perennials, vigilance must also be observed to see that energy is not expended in producing unwanted seeds. After allowing the ripening of whatever small number of seeds is needed for further propagation purposes, remove the rest as they form so that all remaining nutrition will go toward strengthening and enlarging the plant.

Perhaps this is thwarting nature's program. However, do not be deterred but concentrate instead on directing, controlling and enjoying your plants.

In pursuing plant husbandry it would be helpful to know what happens to water and fertilizers that are applied and how they are affected by the environment in which the plant grows. Whatever is applied to any given plant, it is of most help to it as the temperature rises—starting from the coldest point that the plant can tolerate. An Alpine edelweiss that normally blooms even while there is snow on the ground is triggered into growth and can absorb and benefit from nutrients at lower temperatures than species native to the tropics. It is true of almost all species that the warmer daytime hours provide the best conditions for the absorption of nutrients and the plant's ensuing growth. Keeping one's plants in good health requires an almost unconscious but constant appraisal of their state of health. A casual look at a plant that has a rich, dark green color, is producing new growth and is forming flower buds, tells us immediately that all is well. If leaves are dropping or drooping, are mottled or disfigured, a further investigation will uncover the problem. Each deficiency, whether chemical or environmental, will reflect itself in a classic manner, so it is the awareness of any deviation from "normal appearance" that must precede the remedy.

When well fed, plants put on growth that can be pruned, creating compact tree-like forms. This is particularly true of those with woody stems. Herbs such as sentolina, rosemary and tarragon are good candidates.

How Fertilizers Work

Just as the supply of specific chemicals controls the growth and functioning of certain parts of the human body, plants are equally dependent upon many of the same chemicals for their well being. There are two camps, however, each advocating its theory as to "the best way" to feed plants—organically or inorganically. Actually, a plant can only absorb chemicals in solution and whether the chemical is produced artificially, through a manufacturing process or found naturally in some organic form (animal manures, plant composts, etc.), it is virtually the same chemical which is utilized by the plant. True, chemicals can burn plants if

not used in the recommended strengths. Fresh manure will do the same. For the suburban greenhouse owner, the acquisition, storage and use of inorganic (chemical) fertilizers is usually the easiest approach. While fertilizers are formulated in any variety of combinations, a complete fertilizer is basically one that contains nitrogen, phosphorus, potash and trace elements. The first three are always expressed on the container in terms of percentages. Each of these major chemicals control specific plant functions: nitrogen produces more leaf growth, phosphorus, through protein development will help in the development of fruits and flowers, while potash controls vigor and disease resistance. Each of the trace elements (iron, boron, manganese, zinc, etc.) is essential but is needed in relatively small quantities.

Be a Diagnostician

But do not consider the addition of fertilizer as a panacea. First, ask yourself the following questions. The answer to your plant health problem might reveal itself in using this systematic approach:

1. Is there proper drainage?
2. Is there any evidence of insect damage
3. Should the plant be resting or in active growth?
4. Is the artificial climate equal to the plant's native environment?

If each of the above can be eliminated as the source of the problem, *then* consider the application of a moderate amount of a complete fertilizer such as 10-10-10 or 15-30-15. We usually think of plant diseases as of bacterial or insect origin; however, *anything* that affects normal growth can be described as a disease. Therefore, a nutritional deficiency or imbalance of water, light, air and temperature can also be precisely described as a disease problem; so, before treating a plant for a bacterial or insect disease, explore the possibilities of origins more closely associated with daily maintenance. That having been done, let us look further. Bacterial disease covers a wide field, roughly divided into funguses and viruses. The former are often identifiable through a visual examination. Rusts, mildew spots and wilts are spread by airborne spores but can be controlled with a fungicide spray. Viruses can also be seen, some as colorless streaks on the leaves. Since viruses are very difficult to cure it is far simpler to isolate or destroy an infected plant.

Left, *gardenia deficient in iron.* Right, *two weeks later, after application of chelated iron.*

Symptoms of chemical deficiencies are shown in geraniums. Top row shows upper leaves; bottom row, lower leaves. Left column: *shows well-balanced growth.*

Second column: *nitrogen deficiency creates progressively smaller leaves, yellowing until plant succumbs.*

Third column: *upper leaves appear excessively dark due to purple cast created by phosphorus deficiency. Lower leaves gradually die.* Fourth column: *when deficient in potassium, leaves crinkle at extremes with top and bottom leaves fading simultaneously.* Fifth column: *when manganese is in short supply, leaves can not produce chlorophyl and begin dying at bottom of plant.*

Loss of color between the veins as shown here center and right, is called chlorosis and occurs when the plant is short of manganese.

Every bag of complete fertilizer must show the percentage of nitrogen, soluble phosphoric acid and the available potash it contains.

Deformed flowers and discoloration are created by fusarium, a fungus disease.

A soluble fertilizer can be applied automatically through a hose siphon when plants are watered.

Low soil fertility has a debilitating effect as shown by petunia to right of well-fed plant.

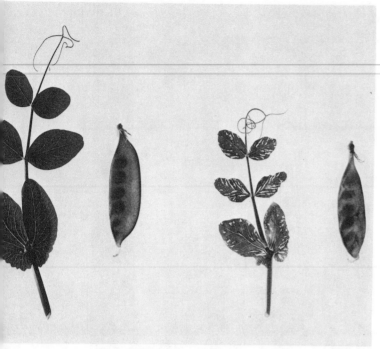

Virus is often indicated by streaks and areas lacking in color such as the pea pod and leaves to the right.

Virus effects upon orchid leaf.

Fast-spreading, powdery mildew begins in a few small areas.

When leaves are kept dry by such means as these chicken wire supports which keep them off the soil, fungus attack can be avoided.

Control of Insects

Insect damage is often seen only when the plant is so severely affected that the control measures are equally damaging. Far more desirable is constant surveillance and this means "looking for trouble." Insects most often lodge themselves either on the underside of leaves or at the point where the leaf is attached to the stem. These are sucking insects that drain the plant of its vitality and a plant can appear to wilt and die without any very noticeable damage. Chewing insects, of course, make their presence known and a vigorous offensive can successfully eradicate them. Slugs, snails, beetles and the like will often feed upon the leaves at night and will stay in dark cool places during the day. Favorite hiding places are under flower pots, under the pot rim or in corners of plant benches.

Daily inspection and bimonthly applications of a broad spectrum insecticide are the most effective means of preventing insects from getting a toehold into your plant collection. How-

Covered with a white cottony substance, mealy bugs hide under leaves and suck plant juices.

Slugs (snails without shells) feast on tenderest parts of plants leaving glistening slimy trail.

Snails thrive under the same conditions as slugs and are similarly controlled.

ever, when applying these chemicals, whether on a preventative basis or to irradicate an infestation, the proper equipment can insure your success. Smoke generators are thorough but are dangerous for use in lean-to greenhouses where toxic chemicals can leak into your living areas. Dusters apply chemicals in powder form almost as thoroughly as smoke. Liquid sprayers allow you to combine various chemicals into one solution and apply in one application. For specific information on insect pests, see pages 91–92.

Scale insects cling to stems and leaves and suck juices while protected by their turtle-like shells.

White flies nervously take wing when plant is jostled.

A mottled effect on leaves is often the sign of a red spider infestation.

Plastic strips impregnated with insecticide such as lindane control insects through emission of fumes. Vapona, above, lasts for months.

Insecticides applied in powder form with a hand-cranked duster assure complete coverage of plant.

Lethal insecticides are often applied by smoke generators. They are only useful in freestanding greenhouses.

The respirator should always be on hand for use with chemical sprays and dusts.

10
Methods of Propagation

One of the greatest pleasures in owning a greenhouse is plant propagation. Aside from the sheer miracle of re-creation is the fascination in the many ways in which new plants can be added to your collection. We normally think of seeds as the way to generate new plants but, aside from the conventional varieties of vegetables and those flowers planted for cutting or bedding, most greenhouse plants will result from other methods. There are no hard and fast rules as to which method of propagation is best in each specific situation but, knowing the alternatives and retaining the knowledge gained from each attempt will, in a reasonable time, allow you to make a quicker decision and assure you of a high degree of success.

Seeds are certainly the cheapest way to produce a large number of small plants. Even in buying top quality seeds from a well recognized seed source, the cost will be minimal. First generation seeds, in the case of hybrids, will be dependable. However, saving and subsequently sowing seeds from your own hybrids can be very disappointing, since their ability to reproduce themselves may vary considerably as to color, size and form. The sowing of seeds and treating them so that you can control their germination requires further understanding in order to achieve a dependable result. Whatever phase of plant care we approach, we can only consider ourselves successful when the results are *predictable*. When you are able to predict the results, you have become a gardener.

Once we get to the asexual methods of reproduction (those other than sowing seeds), many new areas of acquisition are opened to us. That attractive spider plant in your doctor's waiting room, the rex begonia in the shoemaker's window or the exotic streptocarpus with which your neighbor took first prize at the spring flower show are all yours for the asking. Most gardeners are generous and even flattered by being asked to share their plants. You will soon be carrying small plastic bags "just in case" a likely subject for cuttings comes to your attention.

Sowing seeds will invariably be successful if the following precautions are observed:

Citrus seeds are large enough to handle, though seeds of some plants, orchids in particular, are dust-like and can only be sown by special methods.

Largest of all seeds, the coconut often floats for miles before settling in the sand to germinate.

Large seeds can be sown in groups of threes in individual containers.

After thoroughly watering a new planting of seeds, a plastic tent will maintain all the necessary moisture until germination takes place.

1. Use a disease-free medium. This can be a sand and peat moss combination, perlite or vermiculite.
2. Maintain a temperature of 70°F. minimum. A heat source at the bottom of the container is preferable.
3. The soil mixture should not be allowed to dry out at any time.

A moist, and therefore soft, seed coat is essential for germination and the growth immediately thereafter.

If a soil and sand mixture is used, it would be a wise precaution to drench the soil a day or two in advance with a "damping-off solution." This will prevent the fungus disease that often affects new seedlings.

Stem Cuttings

A tremendous number of plants can be propagated by rooting stem cuttings. This can be accomplished in a matter of a few weeks in the case of soft herbaceous growth. Woody stems take longer and require an additional step or two to create the callous necessary for the development of roots. Choose stems about 4 to 6 inches in length that are most typical of the species. Remove any flower buds, since they drain the plants of reserve energy. Four or five leaves should be sufficient to produce food for the soon-to-be new plant. Any more than that should be removed.

Divisions

Each plant species has its own habit of growth, whether it be a single stemmed vine or a rosette of leaves emanating from a central crown. There are also those that enlarge themselves by producing new stems around their perimeter. It is this category that can be taken out of its container, cut apart and the resulting three, four or more new individual plants potted separately.

Remove lowest 2 inches of leaves after snipping off a stem no more than 6 inches long.

Moisten coarse sand, insert cutting to cover two nodes and firm sand to provide close contact with stem.

Remove cutting and pot individually when roots are 1 to 2 inches long.

Sterile propagating media such as perlite overcomes the
hazard of fungus diseases common to soils.

A self-contained mini-propagating-bed can be made by
sinking a 2½-inch pot to its rim in the center of a perlite-
filled 8-inch clay bulb pot. Plug the bottom hole of the small
pot with a cork and fill with water. Dust cuttings in rooting
hormones and insert in rooting medium.

When plant clumps fill pot and roots are equally crowded,
divide plant with sharp knife and pot each section individually with fresh soil.

Leaf Cuttings

The rooting of leaves is one of the methods favored by commercial plantsmen for increasing their supply of saleable plants such as African violets, gloxinias and other species with similarly fleshy leaves. When you consider that a large plant might well have fifteen or twenty leaves that it can spare and each can be rooted, potted and grown into a respectable specimen itself within six months, the value of this technique is obvious.

Air Layering

There are any number of reasons that a plant may become leggy. It could have lost its lower leaves through chill or draft; it could be "reaching" for more light or the encouragement of side branching through tip pinching could have been overlooked. But, whatever the reason, it is probably not too late to make the attractive topmost part of the plant into an entirely new entity and even regenerate leaves and branching in the lower part.

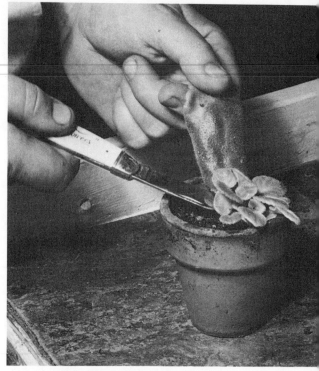

When roots and new leaves are formed, they may be potted and grown individually.

Root fleshy leaves by severing with a short piece of leaf stem, insert to base of leaf in a mixture of coarse sand and peat moss. Cover with plastic until rooted.

Cut stem of leggy plant about halfway through and keep open with matchstick. Blow rooting hormone into wound.

Envelop stem around wound with damp sphagnum moss.

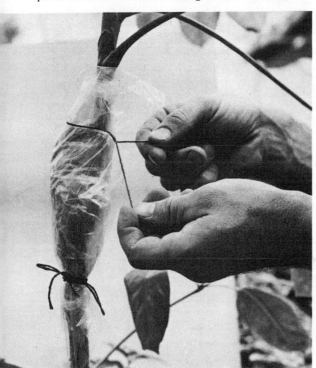

Cover with sheet of polyethylene and tie top and bottom.

In 3 or 4 weeks, there should be sufficient roots to permit severing the new plant on top, to be potted separately and continue feeding and watering the lower part to encourage new branching.

Viviparous Plants

There is a category of plants that produce new plants directly on their stems or leaves. Some even germinate seeds without their leaving the plant. This is called viviparous propagation and for the gardener, it's like picking apples off a tree. A new plant needs only to be put in contact with the soil to continue its root growth. When roots are evident it is no longer dependent upon the mother plant and any connection can be severed.

The tools necessary for plant propagation are few, if any. There are refinements for simple manual actions that save a little time, create a more uniform soil mixture or monitor and perform some functions automatically in your absence. But in all cases these aids must be considered as no more than extensions of your hand. It is this touch and feel that make for an understanding, accomplished gardener.

The viviparous habit of Begonia hispida cucullifera *creates new plants on its upper leaf surface.*

Many species of kalanchoe *form new plants on leaf margins.*

Leaves such as those of Tolmiea menzii *that generate new plantlets on their surface can be held in contact with damp sand with the weight of a stone.*

Roots should form and be about 2 inches long in about 3 weeks.

Severed and potted, the new plant will start branching soon after roots are reestablished.

·A mist-propagation system is a great aid to rooting cuttings quickly. When droplets evaporate on metal "leaf" it lifts, activating the misting nozzles.

Constant moisture during daylight hours helps germination and initial growth. A time clock and solenoid will operate nozzles automatically.

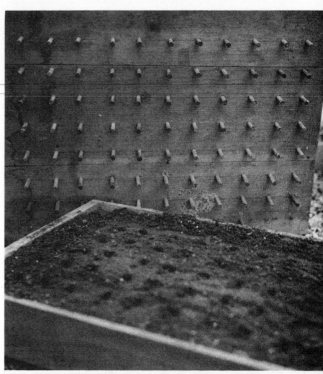

Tamp surface prior to setting out seedlings to insure moisture transmission.

One motion can space holes for transplanting by using a peg board.

Roots should be held in close contact with the soil. Therefore, thorough and gentle watering is crucial.

The bottom warmth of a thermostatically-controlled heat cable aids germination of seeds and the rooting of cuttings.

Any desired soil, from coarse to fine can be separated for use by graduated screens.

*The greenhouse with glass close to the benches is ideal for propagation purposes.
This pit house is also useful in growing alpine plants.*

11
A World of Plants to Choose From

How to Have the Display You Want Exactly When You Want It

Determine your goals and plan an appropriate schedule to avoid a feast or famine kind of greenhouse. There is no point in planting a dozen pots of Easter Lilies if Easter is the time you usually go off on a two-week vacation. First, consider your family's traditional plans over the next twelve months. As sketchy as they may be, you will get some idea of your "home time," "peak entertaining months," vacation periods," etc. Then, knowing the temperature of your greenhouse and its capacity to grow cut flowers as against pot plants, you will be able to make a selection of those plants you would like to grow. Having looked through the following lists of appropriate plants you can figure the time needed for germination, growth to maturity, and time until blooming. These weeks all added together will tell you when to sow the seeds or begin rooting the cuttings in order to have what you want, when you want it.

Choosing Your Plants

You can easily decide what plants you should choose if, in each case, you ask yourself if the temperature needs are compatible with your greenhouse (cool, 45 to 57°F., and warm 58 to 70°F.); is the plant for cut flowers, a pot plant or for summer use in the outdoor garden; is it of manageable size and, if so, how many do you have room for and is it for use as a specimen plant, an accent in a display or as a small "jewel" to be enjoyed from close range?

The world of plants is endless and sometimes it is this tremendous variety of choice that makes a single selection difficult. However, as you gain experience with a few members of a narrow group of plant families you will gain familiarity, experience and confidence and each successive series of choices will be that much easier.

All temperatures shown are Fahrenheit. Following each plant description, C refers to a cool greenhouse and W to a warm greenhouse.

Abutilon megapotamicum—Flowering maple

The decorative hanging flowers of this mallow range from pale yellow through orange to red. Proof that common names are more misleading than a help, this plant is no relation to a maple and only the leaves have any similarity. From tropical Asia, it will do best in a warm greenhouse. Prune it in early spring as new growth begins. C

Allamanda cathartica

A Brazilian vine with funnel-shaped yellow flowers, Allamanda carries an abundance of dark green leaves and the branches are easily trained upon a supportive structure. A minimum 55° temperature, organic soil and an abundance of sunshine and water in its early spring growing season will assure good flowering. Prune in early winter. W

Aloe variegata

The attractively marked leaves make this succulent a good choice for the cool greenhouse in spite of the look of dramatic bloom. The tightly packed rosettes need sparse watering and a coarse, gritty soil. Full sun is preferable both winter and summer. C

Anthurium andreanum

The waxy red spathe and white spadix are as weirdly dramatic as any exotic tropical can be. When not in flower, the dark green foliage is still a very useful foil for other flowering plants. Grow warm, shaded and moist. It will do well under the bench in its early stages of growth. W

Aphelandra squarrosa

Another warm growing top choice. The green and white marked leaves are only slightly less dramatic than the yellow flowers that begin blooming in fall and winter. Grown warm and moist it will provide good color in the greenhouse or can be taken indoors to brighten your house a few days at a time. W

Ardisia crispa

Under its wavy edged green leaves, clusters of bright red berries give this East Indian native its summer desirability. While it starts providing color in May it will continue to do so until fall. It should be kept moist from May til October and then moderately dry during its winter resting period. A 65° summer temperature and 55° during the winter will satisfy its needs. W

Begonia masoniana—Iron cross begonia

While the flower clusters are an attractive pale green, it is the foliage that makes this semi-tropical native a desirable addition to the greenhouse. The surface is uniformly and deeply crinkled and a dark brown marking in the shape of a Maltese Cross is located in the center of each leaf. Organic soil, warm temperatures and moderate but constant moisture will keep this species growing well. W

Begonia rex

The almost endless varieties of leaf colorings and markings make a few of these specimens a *must* in a warm greenhouse to provide a year-round show. An organic soil mixture, daily watering and atmospheric humidity will keep these natives of Assam in almost continuous growth. B. rex 'Mikado' is striking with its purple and silver leaves. B. rex 'Countess Louise Erdody,' with each of its leaves displaying a distinctive whorl, is another that make a good choice in growing these wonderfully colorful plants. W

Begonia tuberhybrida—Tuberous begonia

The flower of this tender plant is so delicate in color and form that it is highly prized as a pot plant. Blossoms may be removed and floated in a bowl of water as a table decoration. Tubers, started in damp peat moss in March at 70°F. will be ready for shallow potting in about one month, when a few leaves have developed.

The delicacy of the blooms of tuberous begonias put them high on the list of beautiful flowering plants.

An organic mixture, daily watering, and dappled light will produce flowers from spring until fall, especially if blooms are removed before they completely fade. Remove the first set of flower buds and, when the next buds develop, pinch out the two small ones (male) on each side of the large central bud which will develop into the extremely decorative female flower. W

Bellis perennis nana—**English daisy**
A few pots of these daisies in mixed color is enough to make any greenhouse worthwhile. They grow easily from seed in a cool greenhouse and a few plants can fit into a 3- or 4-inch pot. Feed with a liquid fertilizer and watch them grow. It is a good gift plant too when visiting friends. C

Beloperone guttata—**Shrimp plant**
A native of Mexico it produces its whitish-pink, shrimp-like flowers from spring to fall. It does best in a cool greenhouse but do not let plants go into the night with excessive moisture. Propagates easily from cuttings in the summer. Pinch tips of branches to promote a bushy habit. C

Bougainvillea spectabilis
Almost everyone knows this tropical vine and since it grows so fast and flowers so heavily, it is a perennial favorite. It will have to be pruned to keep it in control and it can be potted or grown direct in the ground. Stem cuttings root easily and a soil mixture of ⅓ sand, ⅓ soil, ⅓ peat moss and a fistful of bone meal, a temperature of 60° or more and it will soon be a luxurious specimen. C/W

Browallia speciosa var major—**Amethyst flower**
This native of Colombia is most loved for its strong blue daisy-like flowers. It will do well as a pot plant but is especially dramatic in a hanging basket. Its 2-inch flowers are liberally scattered among the small leaves. Two or three plants to a 4-inch pot in a 60° temperature will provide plenty of bloom and seeds sowed at intervals will extend the flowering by several weeks. W

Bromeliads
If you are a new greenhouse gardener, you

In flower or not, a bromeliad planting is always of great interest.

must try growing a few bromeliad species. If you're an experienced greenhouse person you already know the beauty of their flowers, the ease of growing them and the peculiar beauty of their exotic form. Just to zero you in on this plant family, the pineapple is one of its members with which you are, no doubt familiar. The rosette of stiff, and sometimes striped, leaves literally sends its flower spike upward as a firecracker explosion. In addition to the terrestrial pineapple there are scores of epiphytic species as well.

Some bromeliads you might try are:

Aechmea fasciata with its bright pink and blue plume-like flower. W

Aechmea fulgens explodes its purple flowers out of red, berry-like bracts. W

Bilbergia windii guards its drooping flowers with sword-like leaves. C

Cryptanthus fosteriamus is wonderful for its 6- to 8-inch leaves barred with gray-green, brown and red leaves. W

Nidularium innocentii is another with more exciting leaves than flowers. W

These bromeliads can be potted in a mixture of leaf mold and sand or they can be wired to a

The pocketbook plant — Calceolaria herbeohybrida.

supporting tree branch on a piece of cork with a chunk of osmunda wrapped around their roots and a fistful of leaf mold added on top, which will gradually wash into the osmunda.

Caladium candidum

The leaves of these South American plants are striking in their markings, which range from green and white to red and white. Started from tubers in peat moss, kept moderately moist, they will show signs of producing stems after a few weeks in 70° temperature. They can be potted one tuber per pot in rich soil after leaves become evident. Protect from direct sun and they will keep growing new leaves from late winter until fall. W

Calceolaria herbeohybrida—Pocketbook plant

Very popular because of its unusual form and coloration, this cool greenhouse subject will flower in late winter. Seeds germinate best in warmth and after shifting to individual pots, the plants can be grown in a cooler atmosphere. The pouch-shaped flowers, of yellow, red, orange, and a great range of shades in between, last well if air is constantly circulated. A 4- or 5-inch pot will usually contain a well-grown plant 6 inches high. C

Calendula officinalis—Pot marigold

The multipetaled daisy-like flowers are bright and beautiful annuals for the cool greenhouse. Sow seeds in early January and grow in flats for cutting in mid- or late March. Not really marigolds, they have no disagreeable odor. They do have superior, clear oranges and yellows that will make your spring greenhouse come alive. C

Camellia japonica

This is a shrub that will take considerable neglect in its nonblooming months and will slowly begin its new growth in midwinter and start blooming in late March, continuing for many weeks. The individual flowers are tightly packed, multipetaled. Colors range from clear white, red and pink to bicolors of considerable interest. They will progress well on organic acid soil and cool temperatures are best. A little warmth, up to 70°, will be tolerated when it's necessary to speed up the blooming date. C

Chlorophytum comosum var. variegatum—Spider plant

This is an old favorite house plant that will prosper in a moderate temperature of 50°. Its arching stems give rise to new plants at their tips and these can be severed, potted and easily grown into new specimens. A few plants potted in a hanging basket will develop into a striking greenhouse accent in a few months. C

Chrysanthemums

Rooted cuttings, best purchased from specialists, can be selected by variety for growing in hanging baskets, as a cascade, pot plants or for cutting. The latter is grown as a single stem with only the terminal bud being allowed to develop. All the others call for pinching out the grow-tips to encourage multiple stems and the resulting compactness.

Since mums are photosensitive plants and bloom only when days grow short they can be programmed to bloom by creating day length artificially. By keeping lights on an extra few hours each day, vegetative growth can be encouraged. The use of a 60-watt bulb hung 2 to 3 feet above the plants, every 3 feet and hooked up to a time clock will provide this necessary light. In order to initiate the formation of flower buds, absolute darkness must exist for 16 hours (from 4 P.M. to 8 A.M.). This is accomplished by stretching an opaque black cloth over wires running the length of the plant bench. Detailed timing for this process can be supplied for each variety by the producers of rooted chrysanthemum cuttings. C

Cissus antarctica—Kangaroo vine

A most valuable foliage plant, its trailing branches are hidden by 4- or 5-inch deeply cut-edged leaves. Plant rooted cuttings, two or three to a 5-inch pot, pinch tips, water when dry, keep cool and you will soon enjoy its rich green foliage. C

Citrus mitis—Calamondin orange

Buy, borrow or steal a few cuttings of this miniature orange tree and keep transplanting until it is comfortably set in an 8-inch pot. It will grow 2 feet in height. Its waxy white flowers exude an absolutely delicious fragrance and if you never see a fruit, it's still worth growing. If it will not set fruit, use a soft camel's hair brush on the blossoms when the pollen becomes powdery. This manual pollination should bring results. Keep warm and well watered and see that there is plenty of ventilation when flowering begins. W

Cobaea scandens—Cup and saucer vine

This South American vine is tolerant of cool (50°) or warm (65°) temperatures. Its bright purple cup crowns a green calyx which forms its saucer beneath. Sow seeds in February and provide stakes, a trellis or a wall for it to climb upon. It will grow as a perennial but, since it does well from seed, new plants can be grown each year. C/W

Coleus blumei

It is hard to think of this as a Japanese native, since we see it everywhere as a house or greenhouse plant. The foliage is so colorful, with almost no two plants alike if grown from seed, that cuttings are essential if one particular strain is to be perpetuated. Combinations of green, cream, red, orange and yellow predominate. Stem cuttings root so quickly and it forms a compact plant so easily if tips are pinched off periodically that there is no excuse for being

without a coleus. If yours become leggy, make a few new ones and get rid of the old one and provide more light and pinch tips regularly.

Keep warm, moist and provide fresh air. W

Coleus thyrsoideus

This species is recommended exclusively for its flowers. The electric blue color is very special and grown in an 8-inch pot it will develop growth up to 3 feet high and almost as wide. W

Crassula arborescens — Jade plant

This succulent shrub can be grown as a small (3-inch pot) or large (12-inch tub) plant depending upon your available space. From South Africa, it will do well in a cool greenhouse and needs gritty soil. It does flower but the small white blossoms are secondary to the plump, waxy, small ovoid leaves. Cuttings—either stems or leaves—root readily. C

Cymbidium hybrids

This terrestrial orchid has much to recommend it. It flowers dependably, often with several spikes per plant, each spike carrying ten to twenty-five blossoms. Potted in ground-up oak leaves and leaf mold, it should rest (with very little water) in the summer with growth being stimulated in the winter. Flowering will commence in late winter and will remain in good condition (if not pollinated by stray insects) for two months or more. Large plants may be divided with each section repotted in a proportionately smaller pot. C

The diverse forms of bulbs, corms and tubers are only slightly less exciting than their flowers.

Daffodils

It seems that everyone has a mental picture of daffodils and yet each of these ideas can be expanded to include a great many varieties. There are species that produce flowers one-half inch in size and others with large bicolored trumpets. Still others present their flowers in clusters and some are enormously fragrant.

Growing these flowers, as well as many other bulbs in pots, is actually quite simple and very satisfying. Potted in the fall, their roots must be allowed to grow. Then, for about two months they are subjected to a dormant, cold period—an unheated garage is fine. Then, with gradual warmth and an increase in watering they will slowly advance toward flowering. This latter stage can be achieved at a temperature of about 50°. C

Dianthus caryophyllus—Carnation

The pleasing colors and spicy perfume of carnations have made it a favorite cool greenhouse plant. Rooted cuttings can be obtained from a specialist and are best planted at the end of the summer in an organic, slightly alkaline soil. They will do well if adequately ventilated, kept at about 50° and watered early enough in the day to be completely dry by evening. C

Dieffenbachia picta—Dumb cane

A foliage plant of great merit, the green, white and chartreuse markings are most attractive. Although it is capable of reaching 8 to 10 feet in height, it seldom retains enough bottom leaves when it gets tall. Fortunately, *Dieffenbachia* can be propagated easily, either by air layering or by cutting the entire stem into 6-inch sections individually and laying them upon damp sand to root. It needs a slightly moist atmosphere and dappled light. W

Dimorphotheca ecklonis—Cape marigold

This is not a marigold at all but a daisy with pure white rays and a deep blue center. It is a bright and cheerful pot plant and also good for cutting but remember that the flower closes at night. It thrives in organic soil and given bright sunlight will flower abundantly. C

Epiphyllum ackermanni

It is hard to imagine such a weird, tough-looking plant, with flat, scalloped stems, producing such spectacular bright red flowers. If kept dry in winter, when resting, and moist when in growth and at a minimum temperature of 50°, flowering will begin in early spring.

Stem cuttings will root easily if first allowed to callous in the air before inserting in the sand. W

Episcia cupreata hybrids

This is a creeping plant in its native Nicaragua, but there are far more opportunities to use it as a hanging plant in most greenhouses. Such varieties as 'Chocolate Soldier,' with brown and silver leaves are effective even when their bright orange-red flowers are not in bloom. Avoid drafts and water liberally but do not allow soil to become soggy. Stem cuttings will root very easily in a mixture of sand and peat moss in about two weeks. W

Euphorbia fulgens—Scarlet plume

This native of Mexico is a much lesser known relative of the poinsettia. While the flower stems carry less spectacular, small (half-inch) orange-red blossoms, the overall effect of a group of four or five pots is extremely pleasing. Plants can be kept year after year and rested for several months after flowering. The tips of stems should be pinched every month to encourage branching and compactness. W

Felicia amelloides—Blue daisy

This plant is easily grown from seeds or from stem cuttings taken in May. The small leaves are almost obscured by the 2-inch blue rays with yellow centers. These plants are wonderful either as pot plants or in hanging baskets. C

Ferns

Few groups of plants are of greater use to the greenhouse gardener than ferns. While non-flowering, there is a diversity of form among them that makes them useful as a ground cover, in hanging baskets, a foil for flowering plants or as a specimen plant in itself.

Ferns combine well with vines and creepers to naturalize a greenhouse walk.

Davallia bullata

Like many species of this genus, *D. bullata* is most effective in hanging baskets. In this way it is easier to appreciate its hairy rhizomes, often linkened to rabbit's or squirrel's feet. *D. canariensis* is one that can be grown in a cool greenhouse. New plants may be created by germinating spores on the surface of damp sphagnum moss. Spores serve the same function as seeds in flowering plants and may be scraped from the underside of fronds when they are ripe. W

Davallia fijiensis—Squirrel's foot fern

This fern is a perfect greenhouse subject and is best in a hanging basket. In that way its hairy rhizomes are readily seen and its delicate fronds can get plenty of space which, in turn, provides the helpful ventilation. Some shade must be provided to protect it from the full sun and a constantly moist atmosphere is essential. Stem cuttings will root in moist sand if held flat against the surface with a stone or metal staple. W

Asplenium nidus-avis—Bird's nest fern

This fern produces fronds up to 4 feet long and 8 inches wide. They emanate from a central point, creating a rosette of fronds, apple-green in color. This is one that is best used as a specimen plant. W

Dryopteris aemula—Hay-scented fern
—and Polystichum acrostichoides—Christmas fern
—and Athyrium filix-femina—Lady fern

These three very useful ferns for the cool greenhouse can be propagated easily and used to set off the more colorful plants when they're in bloom. C

Ficus benjamina—Fig tree

There are a great many figs that are useful but this tree is a particularly effective foil for flowering plants and the tub can be moved into the house or onto the porch from time to time. It can grow into an enormous tree but takes pruning well so it can easily be kept within bounds. If possible, will benefit from a daily spraying so that its great quantities of 2-inch leaves do not lose excessive moisture. W

Ficus pumila—Creeping fig

This plant will spread and envelop almost anything in its path. It will even cling to glass. Since its tiny 1-inch leaves do proliferate so easily and quickly, it is a particularly good subject to train upon a form such as a chicken wire globe or spire attached to the top of a flower pot. It only needs moisture and some dappled light to become an attractive feature in a few months. W

Fittonia verschaffeltii

With literally hundreds of thousands of potential greenhouse plants, it is extremely difficult to reduce the candidates to a manageable number. However, this is one that just can't be eliminated. While it has an interesting flower spike, it is usually grown for its foliage. The green and crimson veining is most unusual, and you will find the plant useful as a groundcover in the greenhouse. Protect the foliage from direct sunlight to retain the deep colors. W

Freesia

Freesias are the most fragrant member of the Iris family and would be worth growing for the fragrance alone. However these bulbs must be planted for their soft-colored flowers as well. Shades of yellow and orange are particularly pleasing. Pot, root, store and force the same as tulips and daffodils. C

The network of veins of the Fittonia verschaffeltii *compete favorably with other decorative plant forms.*

Fruits and Vegetables

Cucumbers

This vine is best grown upon a trellis in a location that will not cast excessive shade on neighboring plants. A wooden box (about 30 inches long, 12 inches wide and 8 to 10 inches deep) is a good place into which you can transplant four strong seedlings. Water daily and feed with water soluble fertilizer every ten days. Tie vine to trellis with soft twine about every 12 inches. Like most greenhouse fruits and vegetables, you will have to pollinate the flowers when fully open, using a soft camel's hair brush. Syringe the leaves on bright sunny days. Seeds sown in February will produce April fruit. W/C

Grapes

Greenhouse-grown grapes were once fairly commonplace in Great Britain and on the European continent. Now, far too luxurious, it is an effort of love by the amateur—and, after all, the word amateur does mean lover. While grapes were formerly grown in ground beds, they are now best grown in tubs trained upon a single trellis. The black Hamburg, sweet and juicy, is the best dark variety and Seneca is a good white one. Do not grow mediocre varieties since the effort is only worthy of the best. After being cooled in an unheated garage from November until February, bring the tubs into a slightly warmer place. As soon as the buds show signs of developing, increase the watering and syringe the entire stems daily. Remove all the tendrils as they develop and tie the growing branches to the trellis with soft twine or raffia. You will have to pollinate the flowers with a soft camel's hair brush since it will be too early in the season to count on insects to do the job. Once the grapes are of pea size, snip out some if the bunch appears crowded. This will allow the remaining ones to grow large and juicy. Do not try to evaluate the crop in economic terms but enjoy the beauty and form of your vines. If this is not sufficient gratification, then the entire project is one that you can do without.

Lettuce

Of all the varieties Bibb is *the* one. This might sound like a strong opinion—and it is. Bibb is an outstanding crunchy lettuce that grows in tight enough clumps to make one per serving, so it's easy to estimate just how far a particular planting might go. Sow seeds in a 5-inch pot and keep well watered, shaded with newspaper and in a warm (65°) temperature. Provide full light after germination and transplant, well spaced in a wooden flat. Given 6 inches per plant and a 3-inch soil depth, the lettuce plants can be grown and harvested in the flat. C

Few lettuce varieties have the flavor and crispness of Bibb.

Melons

Another effort of dubious value that nevertheless makes a greenhouse seem worthwhile! Seeds should be sown and transplanted as they grow until one or two vines are established in a 6-inch pot. Place each pot on the plant bench close to the glass and train the vine upon a wire stretched overhead. Artificial pollination will be necessary with a camel's hair brush when the flowers are in full bloom. As the melons develop, a net such as a piece of an onion bag should be used as a sling under each melon and tied to the wire to take some of the weight as the melon matures. C

Peas

This vine will bear in March from seeds sown in January, depending upon the number of sunny days. Since peas need bright sunlight they can be grown successfully against the south-facing wall of a lean-to greenhouse. Grown fast, with plenty of water, you will get a quick crop after which you can pull out the vines and replace them with a summer-blooming annual vine such as *Cobaea scandens* or *Thunbergia alata,* started earlier in pots in another part of the greenhouse. C

Tomatoes

Choose the medium size varieties rather than the beefsteaks. They will mature faster and produce a larger crop. Plant a half dozen 6-inch pots, each containing one plant selected as the stoutest ones from a dozen or more grown in a seed pan. One usually thinks of garden tomato plants being bushy and leafy; however, for the greenhouse, train each plant to a single stem tied to a stake. Pinch off the tip of each side branch after it has produced three sets of leaves. The plant, when 5 feet high will look like a column and for additional support, the top can progress from the stake to a wire attached to the greenhouse frame. Once the height has been achieved, pinch out the secondary growth that has begun to grow in the axil of each branch. You are now ready to watch for flowers so that you can pollinate them with your soft camel's hair brush. Seeds sown in February will begin bearing fruit by May. A few good varieties to try are 'Globemaster Hybrid' or 'Gloriana.' Tomatoes will succeed in the cool temperature range of a warm greenhouse or in the warmest part of a cool house. W/C

Fuchsia hybrida

This is a very satisfying cool greenhouse plant that can be grown each year from stem cuttings or can be wintered over in a semi-dormant state year after year and even trained as 4-foot trees in 12-inch tubs. The pink and red or red and white ruffled flowers hang from arching stems that can be pruned to keep them in control. They will become good compact plants if the tips are pinched out periodically after the cuttings are rooted. This is usually in January. Their first few months they should be kept in a warm environment, being exposed to 50 to 55° only after the branching has been well developed. C

Gazania splendens

The daisy-like flowers of this South African annual are now available in a growing variety of yellows, reds and oranges. Seeds may be sown in January for May bloomings. Warmth is needed for germinating and cooler temperatures will suffice after established in individual pots. Flowers close at night so be careful not to use them for dinner table arrangements. C

Gloriosa rothschildiana—Glory lily

The wavy-edged reflexed petals of the flowers of this vining tuberous root are a brilliant red and yellow. Allowed to climb upon a greenhouse wall or on a wire support, the color will be a welcome accent. Start growth in February in a warm greenhouse. After it stops flowering, allow the vine to rest until the following February in a dry, cool place, moistening only enough to prevent shriveling. W

Hedera helix hybrids—English ivy

This plant is so versatile and appears in so many attractive forms that an entire cult of enthusiastic growers has sprung up around this genus. The large-leaved, dull green ivy found at the university and on church walls is the procreator of the scores of cultivars which have sprung to life and have been propagated as named varieties. A few of the outstanding ones are 'Needlepoint,' 'Curlilocks,' 'Shamrock,' and 'Fernleaf.' They may be grown as a groundcover or flowing over the sides of a clay

Small-leafed varieties of ivy lend themselves to all sorts of whimsical forms when trained upon wire framing.

A few months growth will produce a respectable specimen, covering its support wires completely.

pot. The small-leaved ones are particularly adaptable to training upon wire forms. They will respond to a foliar feeding every two weeks. C

Hippeastrum aulicum—Amaryllis

This Brazilian native, like African varieties is a very popular bulb for winter forcing. Potted in a container having adequate depth but sparse side room, it should be given increasing quantities of water, light and warmth. By December, blooming should begin, and by staggering the forcing of individual pots, it is possible to have a few pots in bloom virtually all winter long. The large, brightly colored trumpets open before the full growth of the leaves so that the tall (18 inch) thick stem is rather dramatic, capped by its brilliant two or three flowers—each about 5 inches across.

A 60° temperature is ideal, with fresh water provided daily. After flowers fade, keep up watering daily until the foliage begins to yellow. Then reduce water gradually until foliage browns completely. Cut off dead foliage and keep bulb in the pot in a cool, dark, fairly dry location until ready to top-dress with fresh soil and force into growth once again in the late fall. C

Kalanchöe blossfeldiana

This succulent is a favorite of the cool greenhouse gardener. It can be grown from seeds in the spring and by winter a good size plant—about 6 inches tall—can be flowered in a 6-inch pot. Good ventilation is most important. The soil should be dry before rewatering. W

Manettia bicolor—Firecracker plant

This South American vine will trail as easily as it will climb so a hanging basket makes a fine way to enjoy it. The 1-inch red and yellow tube-like flowers look for all-the-world like firecrackers against the dark green background of their foliage. While cuttings should be kept at 65 to 70° when rooted in the spring, they will do nicely in cooler temperatures as they flower in summer and fall. Tree plants, each grown against a bamboo stake in a 6-inch pot, will form an attractive cone if the tips of the stakes are tied together.

Maranta leuconeura var. kerchoveana—Prayer plant

A foliage plant of far more striking proportions than its 6- to 8-inch height would indicate. The dark green blotches on a lighter green field repeat themselves, creating a unique pattern. A native of Brazil, *Maranta* needs warmth and plenty of water during its growing season. Cooler and drier conditions are best when growth is at its ebb. Propagation by divisions is recommended and this can be done almost any time, repotting into a richly organic soil. W

Medinilla magnifica

A rather large (3- to 5-foot) shrub from the warmth of the Phillipines, this plant would merit growing for its foliage alone. However, the coral-red flowers that bloom in drooping clusters are a bonus not to be ignored. If you have room, beg a cutting to root in a mixture of peat moss and sand. It is well worth adding to a collection in a warm greenhouse. W

Miltonia vexillaria—Pansy orchid

The colors in which this charming South American native is available grows with each year's crop of hybrids. It should be grown in a shaded, fairly moist atmosphere during the summer when it is in most rapid growth. The plant should rest during the winter with a 50 percent reduction in the water applied. Repot in early spring using two-thirds osmunda fiber and one-third sphagnum moss (fresh if possible) to hold moisture. In spite of this absorbent material, provide good drainage and add a few pieces of charcoal to prevent a sour condition from developing. C

Osmanthus fragrans—Sweet olive

This Himalayan shrub can grow over 10 feet tall, but fortunately will survive hard pruning and therefore is easy to keep under control. Its great attraction is the magnificent fragrance of its flowers and, fortunately, it will flower when 6 inches high in a small pot, as easily as a large plant. In either case the fragrance will fill the entire greenhouse in spring and summer. It can be rested during the winter by holding back the full supply of water and giving it a little shade. C

Paphiopedilum insigne—Lady slipper

This orchid species bears flowers that are apple-green in color with purple spots and white edging. They bloom during the winter and remain in good condition well over a month. Paphiopedilum requires a porous growing medium such as that provided in a mixture consisting of equal parts of leaf mold, peat and osmunda. Water thoroughly and then allow the potting medium to dry out before watering again. A cool greenhouse is necessary for the successful raising of those varieties with plain green leaves. Those with mottled leaves require warm greenhouse conditions in order to grow well. C/W

The Medinilla magnifica *is truly an aristocrat of the tropical plant world.*

The Miltonia orchid is called the pansy orchid with good reason.

Passiflora caerulea—Passion flower

Not only are the vine and foliage of this species attractive but the flower is always a greenhouse feature when in bloom. Predominantly strong blue in color, its construction is as symmetrical as it is intricate. It is particularly effective trained on a wire so that it forms an arch across the greenhouse. It is easy enough to cut back, wire and all, after its growing season. This species originates in the South American tropics and does best in organic soil and a warm moist atmosphere. Stem cuttings will root easily in half peat moss and half sand. Watch for wooly aphids and spray monthly with a systemic spray as a preventative measure against insects. W

Pelargonium—Geranium

This genus has captured the admiration of a vast audience and there are many greenhouse enthusiasts who devote their efforts exclusively to growing the various species and hybrids within this genus. In general, geraniums require a cool, sunny greenhouse—even dirty glass will keep them from flowering well. The daytime temperature can go in the 80's before the house is ventilated, but the night temperature should not exceed 55°.

One might think of geraniums in terms of the one type usually seen in window boxes; however, the differences are great indeed. There is a whole group of fancy-leaved varieties with bands of colors ranging from rose to ivory with any number of different greens. There is still another group that is coveted by collectors and that features the fragrant-leaved varieties. Ones with aromas such as nutmeg, orange, coconut, lemon, rose and peppermint are currently available among others. Ivy-leaved geraniums such as 'L'Elegante' or 'Jean Roseleur' are wonderful to grow in hanging baskets or trailing over the sides of raised pots or decorative urns.

Whatever the kind of geranium you grow the plants should be allowed to dry out thoroughly between waterings. C

Peperomia sandersii

Although a tropical plant, this species does well in a dry atmosphere. Its attractively marked leaves are the feature rather than its flowers. If stem cuttings are rooted in the warmth of the summer you will have a good supply of attractive plants in 4-inch pots for the winter, at which time they will tolerate temperatures as low as 55°. W

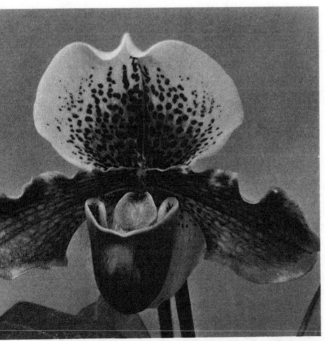

Paphiopedilum hybrid flowers display a rare waxy texture.

Fancy-leaved geraniums are greatly varied and the plant collectors are growing almost as fast as the plant varieties.

Pilea cadierei—Aluminum plant

Silver and green striped leaves are certainly unusual in the plant world, making this a very popular choice. It responds well to tip-pinching, encouraging a bushy, compact habit. An 8-inch plant in a 4-inch pot is easy to achieve in four months from cuttings rooted in a warm atmosphere using a sandy soil mixture. W

Plumbago capensis—Leadwort

The common name of this South African clambering plant is sufficiently unattractive to keep it off the list of any new greenhouse gardener. However, if tried, it will soon become a favorite. Its light blue phlox-like flowers add a soft coloring to the summer greenhouse. Grown from seed in winter, plants can be carried over in subsequent seasons if large ones (6 feet or more in height) are wanted. They will do well in bright sun and can do with a minimum amount of watering all summer when they will bloom continuously until fall. The 8- or 12-inch tub can be stored over the winter in low light, with little humidity and down to 40° temperature. C/W

Primula kewensis

This primula is not as popular as the more colorful *P. malacoides* but its soft yellow florets and white powder dusting over the surface of its leaves make it quite special in its own right. It seeds itself so readily that after the first year's sowing, you will be able to pot up seedlings found on the plant benches in each following year. A single plant centered in a 4-inch pot will spread its whorl of leaves beyond the rim and the flower spikes will hold its clusters of bloom about 5 inches high. C

Saintpaulia ionantha—African violet

Like peanut butter and jelly this plant has been taken to heart in the United States and there are few homes with plants that do not include this one. They bloom almost year round and the colors range from white through pink to deep purple with curly flowers on some and curly leaves on others. African violets need atmospheric moisture and they will also benefit from monthly feedings. The flowers are held but a few inches above its rosette of leaves and, while the pot seems to be full of leaves,

African violets are not easily divided, but are best propagated from leaf cuttings—at any time of the year. The native plants in Tanzania are not nearly so attractive or luxuriant in their growth as those grown in the artificial environment of our greenhouses. W

Senecio cruentus—Cineraria

The single row of petals of brilliant color with a contrasting center make this a "show stopper." This daisy-like native of the Canary Islands is started from seed in July and treated as other biennials, such as pansies. It will advance in growth until it flowers in January. A well-grown plant will need a 5- to 7-inch pot and will produce a mass of color 14 to 18 inches across until late March. It must be provided with good ventilation avoiding drafts, and given a thorough watering daily. C

Sinningia pusilla

This diminutive species is closely related to the better known gloxinia and is similarly grown. It is really a gem. Each flower is about ¼ inch in size, with the entire plant being about 1 inch across. Grown in "thumb pots," sunk to their rim, the individual pot can be brought into the house for display when in bloom. Grown in a humid atmosphere the flowers will reseed themselves and new plants will keep springing up. W

Solanum pseudo-capsicum—Jerusalem cherry

The cherry-like berries (related to the tomato), covering a 12-inch plant, make this a popular winter pot plant. In order to have a good specimen for December, seeds must be sown in the previous February. Transplanted as they grow, plants in 4-inch pots should be summered outdoors, sunk to their rims, and by fall should be in their final 6- or 7-inch pot. Put back in the greenhouse before frost, the berries will begin to show color and will be useful for display over a long period, from late November through February. C

Sophronitis grandiflora

A Brazilian orchid of the cooler high altitudes, this species is rather small (under 8 inches in height) and produces a bright red flower in February. An epiphyte, it is at home

Few flowers evoke the astonished reactions of viewers as much as Cineraria.

The Sinningia pusilla *is one of the daintiest and most dependable flowering plants.*

wired to a slab of tree fern as well as potted in osmunda or fir bark. Like many other orchids, its flowers have extremely good lasting qualities, remaining in colorful full bloom for several weeks. C

Stephanotis floribunda—Madagascar jasmine

This climbing plant is best loved for its extremely fragrant waxy-white tubular flowers. It will tolerate temperatures as low as 50° but does best at 60° and, in the summer, is helped along by daily syringing. In a cool house, grow it against a wall facing south. Like most vines it should be inspected periodically for signs of insects. C/W

Streptosolen jamsonii

There are certain plants chosen for growing into spectacular hanging baskets. This is one. Its orange flowers add wonderful color to the midsummer greenhouse. It responds well to tip pinching and therefore is useful for training as a standard (small tree) if kept predominantly as a single stem until it is 4 feet high. Then, pinch out the growing tip and force the top into a bushy, compact shape. It can also be trained upon a wall if given some support and tied when branches become long. C

Thunbergia alata—Black-eyed vine

An excellent annual vine with unusual brown and orange flowers, it can be trained upon wires or stakes. It is a fast grower in a warm greenhouse but will tolerate temperatures down to 55°. Since it is not a heavy leafed plant, it is best to sow 3 seeds in a 6-inch pot and train each to a bamboo stake forming a cone. It is not a fussy plant and will grow in almost any soil and is not bothered by any specific insects. W

Tibouchina semidecandra—Glory bush

This Brazilian shrub can grow up to 8 feet in height or, by pinching, it can be formed into a nice manageable pot plant in a 6-inch container with branches about 2 feet high and 1½ feet wide. The ovate leaves are of an attractive texture and the royal purple 3-inch flowers are in a class by themselves. While eye-catching, they fit in with almost any other garden colors. Stem cuttings root readily and therefore you

Solanum pseudo-capsicum *is a wonderfully cheerful fruiting plant for the winter.*

might find it more practical to make new plants each year, discarding the large ones after they have bloomed and cuttings have been taken. C/W

Tradescantia fluminensis var. variegata— Wandering Jew

Another of the many Brazilian plants, this creeper is particularly well suited to growing in a hanging basket. Keep pinching the stem tips every few weeks to produce a dense growth of leaves. Then they can be permitted to lengthen and a fine specimen will be established within a year. Well worth the wait. Cuttings root quickly in damp coarse sand. W

Tropaeolum majus

This climber from Peru is more often thought of as a nice little garden flower; however, it is far more attractive as a bush screening plant in the greenhouse. Trained upon a trellis or over any architectural member of the greenhouse it will soon become a mass of green, accented by large orange flowers. Seeds sown in early April will develop well by summer and last until fall. Provide full sun and feed every three weeks with a water soluble fertilizer. C

Tropaeolum tricolor

This tuber is not always easy to buy but the hunt is worth the effort. This is a Chilean miniature, producing a tiny brightly tricolored flower among equally small leaves and, in a 5-inch pot, it is a delightful vignette. Pot the tubers, individually in late summer, for winter bloom. When through flowering, store in a cool, dry location and repot the following August. C

Tulips

Both the species and hybrids are highly gratifying for the brilliance they bring to the winter greenhouse. The flower forms vary greatly including lily-flowered, parrot, double, and large single Darwins. All, however, are grown similarly with the bulb being potted (and they may be crowded with no adverse effect) in October. Keep shaded, cool and watered for about three weeks to allow root growth and then store them where they *can* freeze. Cover them with sand or salt hay once they are frozen but do not allow any rain to reach them or they will be so solidly frozen that removal will be impossible. The coldest area of an unheated garage is a good location for this period. Starting in January, take out a few pots at a time and force them gradually with increasing temperature, light and waterings. Do not force too quickly or the flowers will not last once they open. C

Veltheimia viridifolia

One may get a bit bored by the conventional bulbs and the challenge of a new genus can be stimulating. *Veltheimia* is unusual, with its cluster of tubular flowers forming somewhat of a "foxtail" on its single 12-inch stem. Most are greenish in color but there are hybrids whose flowers are yellow and orange. Each bulb should be potted in a 5-inch pot using a porous soil mixture with the top half of the bulb exposed. C

Zantedeschia aethiopica—Calla-lily

Unusual in form and pristine in color the calla is in a class by itself. It is a large plant, needing a 12-inch tub, and benefits from a thorough daily watering to produce the large leaves which feed the plant. The 8-inch funnel-shaped flowers are carried upon heavy, fleshy stems. There are miniatures and even some species that produce yellow flowers but all are of the same culture. Start them into growth in September. They will flower in December, and, when they cease flowering, continue daily waterings for an additional three weeks. Then, ease off the daily watering allowing the foliage to die down. Keep them dormant for four months before starting them into growth again. C

Other Plants to Grow in a Warm Greenhouse

Acalypha hispida
Achimenes
Adiantum cuneatum
Adiantum peruvianum
Adiantum trapeziforme
Aechmea fasciata
Aechmea fulgens
Aglaonema roebelinii
Anthurium andreanum
Aphelandra squarrosa
Ardisia crispa
Aristolochia elegans
Asplenium nidus-avis
Asplenium viviparum
Begonia socotrana
*Begonia tuberhybrida
*Billbergia windii
*Bouvardia humboldtii
Browallia speciosa var.
   major
Brunfelsia calycina
Caladium candidum
*Campanula isophylla
Cibotium glaucum

Cissus discolor
Citrus mitis
Clerodendrum
   thomsoniae
*Clivia miniata
Coccoloba uvifera
Codiaeum variegatum
   var. pictum
Coelogyne cristata
Columnea gloriosa
Cryptanthus fosterianus
Davallia bullata
Davallia elegans
Dipladenia sanderii
Eucharis grandiflora
Euphorbia pulcherrima
Ficus elastica
Ficus lyrata
Grevellia robusta
Gynura aurantiaca
Gynura sarmentosa
Hibiscus, rosa-sinensis
Ixora coccinea
Jacobinia carnea

Jasminum officianale
   var. grandiflorum
Nelumbium nelumbo
Nidularium innocentii
Passiflora
   quadrangularis
Passiflora trifasciata
Pentas lanceolata
Peperomia caperata
Peperomia obtusifolia
   variegata
Peperomia ornata
Phoenix roebelinii
Platycerium grandis
Poinciana pulcherrima
Russelia equisetiformis
Sinningia speciosa
Spathiphyllum
   clevelandii
Strelitzia reginae
Trachelospermum
   jasminoides
Tradescantia
   fluminensis variegata
Tripogandra multiflora

Plants For Hanging Baskets

*Campanula isophylla
Columnea gloriosa

Platycerium grandis
Russelia equisetiformis

Tradescantia multiflora

Foliage Plants

Adiantum cuneatum
Adiantum peruvianum
Adiantum trapeziforme
Aglaonema roebelinii
Aphelandra squarrosa
Ardisia crispa
Asplenium bulbiferum
Asplenium nidus-avis
Asplenium viviparum
Begonia socotrana

Caladium candidum
Cibotium glaucum
Coccoloba uvifera
Codiaeum variegata var.
   pictum
Cryptanthus fosterianus
Davallia bullata
Davallia elegans
Echeveria gibbiflora var.
   metallica

Ficus elastica
Ficus lyrata
Grevellia robusta
Gynura aurantiaca
Gynura sarmentosa
Peperomia caperata
Peperomia obtusifolia
   variegata
Peperomia ornata
Phoenix roebelinii

Vines

Aristolochia
   elegans

Cissus discolor
Jasminum officianale

   var. grandiflorum
Platycerium grandis

*Will grow in either a cool or warm greenhouse.

Other Plants for the Cool Greenhouse

Acacia armata
Adiantum pedatum
Agapanthus africanus
Aloe variegata
Arum creticum
Arum palaestinum
Azalea indica
*Begonia tuberhybrida
*Billbergia windii
Bomarea kalbrayerii
Bougainvillea glauca
Bougainvillea spectabilis
Bouvardia humboldtii
*Bromeliaceae—see
   Bromeliads
Calceolaria
   herbeohybrida
Camellia japonica
*Campanula isophylla
Campanula pyramidalis
Cephalocereus senilis
Cestrum aurantiacum
Chrysanthemum hybrids
Cissus antarctica
Clianthus dampieri
*Clivia miniata
Coryphantha arizonica
Crinum powellii
Cyclamen persicum var.
   giganteum
Cymbidium 'Flirtation'

Cymbidium 'Peter Pan'
Cyperus alternifolius
Cyperus papyrus
Daphne odora var.
   marginata
Datura suaveolens
Dendrobium nobile
Dicentra spectabilis
Echinocactus grusonii
Echinocactus sarcocaulis
Exacum affine
Fatshedera lizei
Freesia hybrida
Grevillea robusta
Haemanthus coccineus
Haemanthus katherinae
Heliaporous mallisonii
Heliotropium
   arborescens
Heliotropium rutilum
Hibiscus coeleste
Hippeastrum pratense
Hoya carnosa
Hyacinth
Lachenalia tricolor
Lagerstroemia indica
Lapageria rosea
Miltonia vexillaria
Mimulus glutinosis
Narcissus
Nemesia strumosa

Nerine sarniense
Nerium oleander
Notocactus mammulosus
Nymphaea tetragona
   helvola
Oxalis bowiei
Oxalis cernua
Oxalis crassipes
Oxalis rubra
Pelargonium
   coriandrifolium
Pelargonium
   dasycaule
Pelargonium
   domesticum
Pelargonium 'Lady
   Washington'
Pelargonium peltatum
Palargonium
   tetragonum
Salpiglossis sinuata
Schizanthus hybrids
Schizostylis coccinea
Selaginella kraussiana
Soleirolia soleirolii
Torenia fournieri
Trachelospermum
   jasminoides
Tropaeolum majus
Tropaeolum tricolor
Zantedeschia aethiopica

Plants For Hanging Baskets

*Begonia tuberhybrida
*Campanula isophylla

Cissus antarctica
Heliaporus mallisonii

Hoya carnosa
Pelargonium Ivy-leaved
Tropaeolum majus

Foliage Plants

Adiantum pedatum
Fatshedera lizei

Grevillea robusta
Selaginella kraussiana

Vines

Bougainvillea
   spectabilis
Hoya carnosa

Lapageria rosea
Tropaeolum majus
Tropaeolum tricolor

Glossary

Break—development of a new stem at a node or leaf joint.

Compost—organic matter which has partially decomposed.

Damp-down—to spray walkway or underbench area with water; done to raise the humidity and lower the temperature.

Damp-off—the rotting of stems and wilting of leaves of young seedlings due to a fungus disease. Pasteurizing soil or drenching soil with a commercial damp-off solution prior to sowing seeds will help ward off infection.

Disbudding—removing axillary buds so that a terminal bud can develop fully.

Dormancy—the period when a plant shows no apparent growth, brought about by seasonal changes in temperature and humidity.

Epiphytic plants—those that grow on trees and have their roots exposed to the air. Their nourishment comes from both the air and decayed organic matter such as dead leaves that are blown against the roots but no nourishment is derived from the host plant.

Flaccid leaves—those wilted or limp, indicating insufficient water.

Flat—a wooden box, approximately 12 x 24 x 3 inches, into which seedlings are transplanted. Smaller flats of plastic and papier-mâché are also available from horticultural supply houses.

Forcing—accelerating the natural sequence of growth. Sometimes forcing follows an artificially induced dormancy or growth stimulus.

Friable—workability of the soil, when it is somewhat crumbly to the hand.

Genus—to a plant, what a surname is to a person. Those plants that are closely related fall into one genus. The plural is genera.

Hardening-off—the process by which soft plant tissue is gradually acclimated to cooler outdoor temperatures after it has developed soft and tender growth in the greenhouse. This is done by placing the plant in a protected location (like a cold frame) which, although still covered, ·will provide less heat than heretofore, prior to its being completely exposed to the outdoor environment. Eliminating this step may result in losing your plants if the weather turns cold.

Hardy plants—those which survive the winter in a particular area. Knowing the minimum winter temperature in that area (which may be its native area) will enable you to determine its hardiness or ability to survive the winter in another locale.

Internode—the space between the joints on the plant stem. When there is insufficient light the internodes may become elongated.

Leaching—the process of removing chemical ingredients in the soil by the flow of water through it. This is sometimes done deliberately to get rid of excess nitrogen or soluble salts but, usually it is done inadvertently, and depletes the helpful materials, which then must be replaced.

Nodes—the joints on a plant stem where leaves or other stems may grow.

Offset—a bulblet or a new plant growing from the side of the parent plant. As soon as roots form, the offset can be cut apart and potted individually.

Pan—a shallow pot used for growing bulbs, ferns, or any of those plants that grow best with their roots at moderate depth.

Parasitic plant—one that gets its nourishment from the host on which it grows. Orchids do not fall into this classification (see Epiphyte).

Pinching or stopping—technique to encourage branching and produce a bushier compact plant by pinching out the growing tip of the main stem. This is done after the development of the second or third set of leaves.

Plunging a pot—burying a pot of bulbs over its rim in sand outdoors during the fall and winter while it develops a root system prior to its becoming dormant. In the summer some greenhouse plants are plunged outdoors in the garden to continue their growth without daily watering being needed.

Pot-bound—a plant whose roots fill the pot and, in some cases, also grow over the entire surface of the soil. Some plants, such as amaryllis, agapanthus, and geranium, flower best when pot-bound. Others such as chrysanthemum, fuchsia, and gloxinia need room for their active and finer-textured roots to feed.

Potting on—moving plants to progressively larger individual pots as they grow.

Pricking-out—the transfer of seedlings (having already acquired their true leaves) from a crowded seed pot to better spacing in a wooden flat.

Rest—although a plant may be planted in a geographically foreign location, its internal calendar maintains a predetermined cycle during a part of which it makes little or no growth. Resting is also a part of the recuperative period, after flowering, prior to active growth.

Species—the epithet, which follows a plant's generic name and refers to a plant which has enough distinct characteristics to set it apart from others in the genus. There are, however, a sufficient number of other similar characteristics to classify it within the same genus. The singular and plural of species are the same.

Standard—a plant grown tree-like, trained to a single stem.

Succulents—plants able to store large amounts of water in their leaves or stems. All cacti are succulents although all succulents are not cacti. There are succulent species of geranium, agave, begonia, haworthia, and ceropegia, to name but a few other than cacti.

Tender plants—those that cannot withstand frost and, therefore, have to be given the protection of a greenhouse in cold regions in order to survive the winter.

Terrestrial—plants that grow with their roots in the soil, as do most of our garden flowers, trees, and shrubs. A large number of orchids are also terrestrial.

Top growth—the production of leaves which feeds the bulb or corm to replenish its energy for future flowering.

Transpiration—involves the loss of water through the leaves. Both air movement and warmth will facilitate this loss.

Viability—the ability of seeds to germinate which is often measured in percentage. The age and conditions of storage play an important role in the viability of seeds.

How to Deal with Pests and Disease

(Not for Use on Fruits or Vegetables)

Problem	Control Material	Form	Per Gallon of Water	Special Precautions or Limitations
Aphids	Malathion	25% wettable powder	5 tablespoons	Not for use on crassulas, ferns or petunias.
	or			
	Diazinon	50% wettable powder	2 tablespoons	Not for use on gardenias or poinsettias.
Bacterial Diseases	Captan	50% wettable powder	2 tablespoons	
Botrytis	Captan	50% wettable powder	2 tablespoons	
Diseases of fungus and bacterial origin	Bordeaux mixture (¼ cup copper sulphate and ¼ cup hydrated lime in 1 gallon of water)			Spray mixture without further dilution.
	or			
	Benomyl	50% wettable powder	1½ teaspoons	
General fungus diseases	Benomyl	50% wettable powder	1½ teaspoons	
	or			
	Zineb	65% wettable powder	1 tablespoon	
Leaf Spot	Maneb	80% wettable powder	2 tablespoons	
Mealy bugs	Malathion	50% emulsion	2 teaspoons	Not for use on cassulas, ferns or petunias.
	or			
	Vapona strips		1 strip for each 1,000 cubic feet of area	Replace strip every 60 days.
Powdery Mildew	Benomyl	50% wettable powder	1 teaspoon	
	or			
	Karathane	25% wettable powder	2 teaspoons	

Problem	Control Material	Form	Per Gallon of Water	Special Precautions or Limitations
Red Spider Mites	Kelthane	18½% emulsion	2 teaspoons	
Rusts	Zineb or	65% wettable powder	1 tablespoon	
	Captan	50% wettable powder	2 tablespoons	
Scale Insects	Malathion	25% wettable powder or	2 tablespoons	
		50% emulsion	2 teaspoons	
Slugs and Snails	Metaldehyde (Slugit, Slug-kill, and Snarol)		Do not dilute. Use as it comes in the package.	Apply weekly for 4 weeks.
White flies	Resmethrin	24.3% emulsion	2 teaspoons	

If you do not feel qualified to make sufficiently accurate insect identifications you might make up an all-purpose insect spray and apply it twice a month as a preventative measure.

Formula for All-Purpose Spray Mixture:

2 tablespoons of Sevin 50% wettable powder
4 tablespoons of Malathion 25% wettable powder
1½ tablespoons of Kelthane 35% wettable powder
Add all three of the above to 1 gallon of water

Sources of Supply

Vendors of Greenhouses and Accessories

Aluminum Greenhouses, Inc.
14615 Lorain Avenue
Cleveland, Ohio 44111

Dome East
325 Duffy Avenue
Hicksville, New York 11801

Glass Garden Greenhouses, Inc.
P. O. Box 2329
Grand Rapids, Michigan 49501

Lord and Burnham
Irvington, New York 10533

National Greenhouse Company
Box 100
Pana, Illinois 62557

J. A. Nearing Co., Inc.
10788 Tucker Street
Beltsville, Maryland 20705

Redfern's Prefab Greenhouses
55 Mt. Hermon Road
Scotts Valley, California 95060

Peter Reumuller, Greenhouseman
P. O. Box 26666
Santa Cruz, California 95060

Stearns Greenhouses
98 Taylor Street
Neponset, Massachusetts 02122

Sturdi-Built Manufacturing Company
11304 S. W. Boones Ferry Road
Portland, Oregon 97219

Texas Greenhouse Co., Inc.
2710 St. Louis Avenue
Fort Worth, Texas 76110

Turner Greenhouses
P. O. Box 1260
Goldsboro, North Carolina 27530

The Vegetable Factory
100 Court Street
Copiague, New York 11726

Accessories and Supplies

George J. Ball, Inc.
West Chicago, Illinois 60185
— seeds, plants, rooted cuttings, greenhouse supplies

Brighton By-Products Co., Inc.
P. O. Box 23
New Brighton, Pennsylvania 15006
— general supplies

Dillon Industries, Inc.
P. O. Box 224
Melrose, Massachusetts 02176
— soil pasteurizers

Florist Products
1843 E. Oakton
Des Plaines, Illinois 60018
— greenhouse supplies

H. P. Supplies
Box 18101
Cleveland, Ohio 44118
— lighting and watering devices

Humex (International) Limited
5 High Road, Byfleet, Weybridge,
Surrey, KT14 7QF, England
— automatic nonelectric watering and ventilating devices, shading devices, tensiometers for measuring need of watering

Walter F. Nicke P. O. Box 71 Hudson, New York 12534	general supplies
Al Saffer and Co., Inc. 130 West 28th Street New York, New York 10001	chemicals and accessories
Shoplite Co., Inc. 566 Franklin Avenue Nutley, New Jersey 07110	fluorescent lighting supplies
X. S. Smith Company Box 272 Red Bank, New Jersey 07701	black cloth for shading chrysanthemums and plastic screening
Sudbury Laboratory, Inc. Box 1028 Sudbury, Massachusetts 01776	soil testing equipment

Vendors of Seeds, Plants and Bulbs

Abbey Garden Box 167 Reseda, California 91335	succulents
Alberts & Merkel Bros., Inc. Boynton Beach, Florida 33435	orchids and other tropical plants
Antonelli Bros. 2545 Capitola Road Santa Cruz, California 95010	tuberous begonias
Armacost & Royston 2005 Armacost Avenue West Los Angeles, California 90025	orchids
Buell's Greenhouses Eastford, Connecticut 06242	African violets, gloxinia, and other gesneriads
W. Altee Burpee Co. Philadelphia, Pennsylvania 18132	seeds of annuals, biennials, and perennials
Butchart Gardens, Ltd. P. O. Box 4010, Station A Victoria, British Columbia	seeds
Fennell Orchid Co. 26715 S. W. 157th Avenue Homestead, Florida 33030	orchids
Fischer Greenhouse Linwood, New Jersey 08221	African violets
J. Howard French Box 37 Lima, Pennsylvania 19060	bulbs
Joseph Harris Co., Inc. Moreton Farm, Buffalo Road Rochester, New York 14624	vegetable seeds

Alexander I. Heimlich 71 Burlington Street Woburn, Massachusetts 01801	miniature bulbs, corms, and tubers
Margaret Ilgenfritz P. O. Box 665 Monroe, Michigan 48161	orchids
Jones and Schully, Inc. 220 N. W. 33rd Avenue Miami, Florida 33142	orchids
Michael Kartuz 92 Chestnut Street Wilmington, Massachusetts 01887	general plants
Logee's Greenhouses Danielson, Connecticut 06239	general plants
Merry Gardens Camden, Maine 04843	general plants
George W. Park Seed Co. Greenwood, South Carolina 29646	seeds
J. A. Peterson 3132 McHenry Avenue Cincinnati, Ohio 45211	African violets
John Scheepers, Inc. 37 Wall Street New York, New York 10005	bulbs
Sunnyslope Gardens 8638 Huntington Drive San Gabriel, California 91775	rooted chrysanthemum cuttings
Thompson & Morgan, Ltd. London Road Ipswich IP2 OBA Suffolk, England	wide variety of seeds of annuals, biennials, perennials, and shrubs
or P. O. Box 24 401 Kennedy Boulevard Somerdale, New Jersey 08083	
Vetterle Bros. P. O. Box 1246 Watsonville, California 95076	tuberous begonias

Index